Turkish–Russian relations

As the two most influential and powerful actors in Eurasia the nature of the Turkish-Russian relationship affects the situation in the Black Sea, South Caucasus, Central Asia and Middle East and steers the foreign policy formulations of both regional states and global powers. Examining post-Cold War relations between Eurasia's most prominent actors, this book takes into account regional dynamics and global power struggles and identifies three important stages in Turkish-Russian relations during the period. Using complex interdependency theory the author offers valuable insights into the initial confrontational period and its transition to an atmosphere of compromise, cooperation and the evolution of multi-dimensional partnership. Leadership theory then explains the most recent deterioration in rapport as crises in Syria and Ukraine have placed severe strain on the previously warm bilateral relations.

Fatma Aslı Kelkitli is Assistant Professor in the department of Political Science and Public Administration at Istanbul Arel University.

Turkish–Russian relations
Competition and Cooperation in Eurasia

Fatma Aslı Kelkitli

LONDON AND NEW YORK

First published 2017
by Routledge

2 Park Square, Milton Park, Abingdon, Oxfordshire OX14 4RN
52 Vanderbilt Avenue, New York, NY 10017

Routledge is an imprint of the Taylor & Francis Group, an informa business

First issued in paperback 2019

Copyright © 2017 Fatma Aslı Kelkitli

The right of Fatma Aslı Kelkitli to be identified as author of this work has been asserted by her in accordance with sections 77 and 78 of the Copyright, Designs and Patents Act 1988.

All rights reserved. No part of this book may be reprinted or reproduced or utilised in any form or by any electronic, mechanical, or other means, now known or hereafter invented, including photocopying and recording, or in any information storage or retrieval system, without permission in writing from the publishers.

Notice:
Product or corporate names may be trademarks or registered trademarks, and are used only for identification and explanation without intent to infringe.

British Library Cataloguing in Publication Data
A catalogue record for this book is available from the British Library

Library of Congress Cataloging in Publication Data
Names: Kelkitli, Fatma Aslı, author.
Title: Turkish-Russian relations : competition and cooperation in Eurasia / Fatma Aslı Kelkitli.
Description: Abingdon, Oxon ; New York, NY : Routledge, 2017. | Includes bibliographical references and index.
Identifiers: LCCN 2016042577| ISBN 9781138218284 (hardback) | ISBN 9781315437934 (e-book)
Subjects: LCSH: Turkey--Foreign relations--Russia (Federation) | Russia (Federation)--Foreign relations--Turkey. | Geopolitics--Eurasia.Classification: LCC DR479.R9 K45 2017 | DDC 327.561047--dc23
LC record available at https://lccn.loc.gov/2016042577

ISBN: 978-1-138-21828-4 (hbk)
ISBN: 978-0-367-26465-9 (pbk)

Typeset in Times New Roman
by Taylor & Francis Books

Contents

List of tables vii
Acknowledgements viii

Introduction 1

PART I
Multiple ties that bind Turkey and Russia 17

1 Flourishing of a multifaceted relationship 19

PART II
The issues of competition and cooperation 33

2 Clashing positions amidst attempts to gain ground in the South Caucasus 35

3 Low-intensity Turkish–Russian rivalry in the Steppes of Central Asia 57

4 Collaboration in the Black Sea 65

5 Sensitive spots: Chechen and Kurdish matters 77

6 The growing gap in the Middle East 86

PART III
Consolidation of economic association   103

7   Broadening and deepening of economic bonds   105

    Conclusion   129

    Index   137

Tables

3.1 Natural gas transportation by years (1987–2015) (million cubic meters)   111

Acknowledgements

Some parts of Chapter 2 were published as an article named "Russian Foreign Policy in South Caucasus under Putin" in *Perceptions (Journal of International Affairs)* 13(4), 2008, by the Center for Strategic Research (SAM), and some parts of Chapter 3 were published as an article named "The Meeting of the Crescent and the Dragon: Post-Cold War Sino-Turkish Rivalry and Cooperation in Central Asia and the Middle East" in the *Journal of Central Asian and Caucasian Studies* 9(17), 2014, by the International Strategic Research Organization (USAK). They reappear here with the publishers' permission.

Introduction

This book examines the post-Cold War bilateral relationship between Eurasia's two prominent and long-standing actors, Turkey and Russia, by taking into account regional dynamics as well as global power struggles that have impact on their interaction. Probing the course of Turkish–Russian rapport is significant due to the fact that these two countries are the most influential and powerful actors in Eurasia by all historical, political, economic and military accounts. For this reason the state of their relationship, its character of being conflictual or cooperational has region-wide implications, affecting the situation in the Black Sea, South Caucasus, Central Asia and Middle East and steers the foreign policy formulations of both the regional states and also of the global focuses of power that has interests and stakes in these regions.

This study will investigate the post-Cold War Turkish–Russian relations by focusing on the two states' association in the fields of politics, economics and security. It is possible to observe three important shifts in the course of Turkish–Russian relations in this era which are defined as problem/goal changes by Charles Hermann (1990, 5). First, the conflictual and confrontational atmosphere of the early 1990s during which Turkey and Russia occasionally tangled over bilateral and regional matters that is to say accusing each other of supporting the separatist forces in each other's territory, squabbling over passage of Russian ships through Turkish Straits and provisions of Treaty on Conventional Forces in Europe, siding with different parties of the conflicts in Bosnia and Herzegovina and Nagorno-Karabakh and backing competitive energy projects, evolved into a climate of moderation and compromise at the end of the decade which resulted in toning down of the mutual complaints and harsh criticisms in addition to the planting of the seeds of lasting cooperation between the two states in the energy field.

Second, the shift from increasing cooperation to multi-dimensional partnership took place in the mid-2000s which was spurred by rising economic and commercial ties between the two countries as well as convergent standings in some regional issues. Concomitant to increasing and diversifying economic ties, Russia and Turkey commenced to see each other not only as rivals that vie for influence in the neighboring regions but also as promising trade partners.

The third change in the relationship came into being on November 24, 2015 when a Turkish F-16 fighter shot down a Russian Sukhoi Su-24M bomber on the grounds of violation of Turkish airspace. The incident which resulted in the death of the pilot in command was described as a stab in the back by Russia which would not be expected from a friendly country. Russia denied the Turkish claim of encroachment of sovereignty and contended that the bomber was acting within the confines of Syrian territory ("Turkey Says Su-34 Violated Airspace" 2016). Moscow quickly took steps to freeze all kinds of political, economic and socio-cultural contacts with Turkey. The highly chafed association showed signs of recovery seven months later only after the Turkish President Recep Tayyip Erdoğan sent a letter to his Russian counterpart Vladimir Putin which expressed his deep regret for what happened (President of Russia 2016) and which led Putin to ease some of the restrictions set on Turkey.

The following part will examine the origins of these three significant shifts in the Turkish–Russian relationship. While the complex interdependency theory offers invaluable insights in throwing light to the roots of the first two changes, it needs to be supplemented with the leadership theory in order to figure out the essence of the last one.

Revealing the underpinnings of the Turkish–Russian interaction in the post-Cold War era

Complex interdependency theory

The first two changes in Turkish–Russian relations are well grasped by the complex interdependency theory that was put forth by Robert Keohane and Joseph Nye in their book *Power and Interdependence: World Politics in Transition*. According to Keohane and Nye, interdependence refers to situations characterized by reciprocal effects among countries or among actors in different countries (1977, 8). Where there are mutual although not necessarily symmetrical costly effects of transactions, there is interdependence. The authors talk about two types of interdependence. The first one is sensitivity interdependence which involves degrees of responsiveness within a policy framework, that is, how quickly changes in one country bring costly changes in another, and how great the costly effects are (1977, 12). In sensitivity interdependence the framework remains unchanged and no new policy is devised due to the difficulty in formulating new policies within a short time or commitment to a certain pattern of domestic and international rules. The vulnerability interdependence is defined as the relative availability and costliness of the alternatives that various actors face (1977, 13). In vulnerability interdependence more alternatives are available and different policies are possible.

The complex interdependency theory has three main hypotheses each of which can be accepted as a challenge to the basic premises of realist theory. The first assumption makes a viable point of the emergence and growing significance of the non-state actors such as intergovernmental organizations, non-governmental organizations (NGOs), multinational corporations and transnational actors in world politics.

The number of intergovernmental organizations increased from 600 in 1980 to over 6,000 nowadays (Keohane 1993, 285; Milner 2009, 6). Some of them, such as the International Monetary Fund, the World Bank and the World Trade Organization proved to be quite capable of subduing states in need of credits, loans and undisputed trade flows to their rules and conditions even if this meant diminution of those states' fiat concerning important financial, economic and commercial decisions. What is more is the vivid example of the European Union (EU) where the member states accepted to cede substantial part of their sovereignty to the institutions of the Union regarding agriculture, trade, monetary and fiscal policies.

The end of the Cold War and the formation of democratic regimes in the former communist countries along with the information revolution which made quick, affordable and efficient communication between individuals in different parts of the globe possible prepared a suitable ground for NGOs to expand and increase their influence. Their number, approximated to 26,000 (Keohane and Nye 2000, 116) in the 1990s, grew to more than 45,000 within a decade (Agg 2006, 1). The NGOs acted as pressure groups on the states and managed to mobilize some segments of the international community around the issues of development, human rights, health, environment, fight against poverty, emancipation of women, immigration, humanitarian aid and the establishment of rule of law and justice. Their struggle and endeavor produced tangible results now and then such as the adoption of the Montreal Protocol on Substances Depleting the Ozone Layer, emergence of the Mine Ban Treaty and the embodiment of the Rome Statute of the International Criminal Court.

The gradual but steady retreat of the state from production, ownership of public enterprises, investment as well as research and development expedited with the prevalence of liberal economic model all around the world in the wake of the end of the Cold War opened up new avenues for multinational corporations to permeate into countries that were completely off-limits to their operations at earlier times. Currently, there exist about 82,000 multinational corporations (United Nations Conference on Trade and Development 2009), functioning with more than 800,000 foreign affiliates scattered around various parts of the world. A multinational company might contribute to a host state's economy through launching diverse and sophisticated products, offering effective and innovative management techniques along with creating job opportunities for the local workforce. In return, it expects significant concessions from the government of the host state which impinge on its domains of power and authority such as less regulated business environment, compliant labor unions and less sensitivity for environmental and safety precautions.

The strengthening and growing influence of transnational actors such as international criminal gangs that are engaged in illegal arm, drug and human trafficking activities, international terrorist organizations which direct deadly attacks on military and civilian targets in many countries and religious groups that proved to be quite adept at distributing aid and resources to its adherents complicate the matters further for the state as they challenge its unique role as chief provider of security and prosperity.

All in all, states which lack requisite political, economic and military wherewithal to cope effectively with the encroachments of non-state actors have to fight tooth and nail to hold their ground in an increasingly complex and competitive international arena. States while carrying on with this struggle do not exist in an isolated environment; they have to communicate, interact and even cooperate with these centrifugal forces. Accordingly, today there exist multiple channels of contact for states including formal and informal ties with the governmental elites and foreign office representatives of the other states as well as formal and informal connections with non-governmental elites.

The second premise of the complex interdependency theory underscores the absence of hierarchy among international issues. Military security does not consistently dominate the agenda (Keohane and Nye 1977, 25), at least except the situations of security dilemma. The distinction between domestic and foreign policy is blurred and economic issues such as economic growth, wealth and welfare of the citizens are becoming as significant as concerns associated with security and survival of the state. This change can be figured out clearly through the examination of post-Cold War resolutions and decisions adopted by the United Nations (UN) General Assembly. The number of the resolutions regarding financial matters, trade, development, food and hunger problems has augmented steadily throughout the years and has finally surpassed the ones concerning security issues such as international terrorism, arms control, disarmament and nuclear proliferation in the last years (United Nations General Assembly 2015).

The last hypothesis of the complex interdependency theory states that except in matters of life and death, recourse to force to solve the international disputes, especially among industrial nations, seems less likely. The destruction capability of nuclear weapons and the popular opposition to prolonged military conflicts in Western democracies made resort to violence less feasible and applicable (Keohane and Nye 1977, 29). Furthermore, there is no guarantee that military methods will be more effective than the economic means to accomplish a certain objective.

The complex interdependency theory manages to draw a more comprehensive and fully fledged picture of the current international environment compared to realism. States are still the primary players in international politics; however, their ability to control and preserve their assumed domains is growing more and more difficult due to the onslaughts of the non-state actors. Moreover, the issues they have to grapple with have increased in number and diversity as well. States are expected to find solutions not only to political and security matters as they did in good old days but also to pressing economic, social, health and environmental problems. Lastly, despite the occasional outbreak of wars and military conflicts, one can also witness many situations where states decide to negotiate and cooperate rather than appeal to military means.

The complex interdependency theory provides important guidelines to understand the reasons of two major changes that took place in Turkish–Russian relationship in the late 1990s and mid-2000s. Starting from late 1990s up until the plane incident of November 2015, Turkish–Russian economic cooperation and political dialogue have reached unprecedented levels. With a trade volume of more than 31 billion dollars in 2014, Russia turned out to be Turkey's second largest trading partner after Germany in accordance with Moscow's becoming of chief natural gas supplier of Ankara. Reciprocal visits at presidential, prime ministerial and ministerial levels became common occurrences. Even the military cooperation, the weakest link of the bilateral interaction, demonstrated some revival as Turkey, after a long interval, decided to buy military equipment from Russia, and the navies of the two states participated in joint surveillance operations in the Black Sea.

Energy relations between the two counties carried both the characteristics of sensitivity and vulnerability interdependence. Turkey was sensitive to the natural gas and oil supplies coming from Russia whereas Russia was sensitive to the hard currency it earned from the lucrative Turkish market. With regard to the oil supplies Turkey had many alternative source countries such as Iran, Iraq, Saudi Arabia and Kazakhstan and this reduced its vulnerability. However, there existed a different situation concerning natural gas imports; Turkey was the more vulnerable party in this trade-off. If Russia ceased to supply natural gas to Turkey, the country would face serious troubles as it lacked sufficient alternative sources to replace the Russian natural gas. Iran, the second major natural gas provider of Turkey after Russia, was not a reliable source country as in preceding years it many times cut off gas supplies to Turkey in the middle of the winter on the basis of domestic consumption priorities, technical problems and explosions in the pipeline. The natural gas export to Turkey from Azerbaijan, Algeria and Nigeria was in meager amounts and could not suffice to satisfy Turkey's all energy needs. Moreover, both Algeria and Nigeria were geographically distant states and Turkey paid high transportation costs while purchasing natural gas from these countries. Russia, on the other hand, would be deprived of a high-potential and profitable market if Turkey declined to buy its natural gas, but the presence of cash-rich clients in Europe and Asia that were eager to buy Russian natural gas would compensate its losses in the Turkish market. So, Turkish–Russian energy interdependence was asymmetrical in nature and Russia, being the less dependent actor, had more bargaining power compared to Turkey as it was less costly for her to break off the relationship in the case of a major discord.

National governments occupied a significant place in Turkish–Russian relations. Over the last decade many high-level diplomatic visits occurred between the two countries. Four presidential level, two prime ministerial level and six foreign ministerial level visits from Russia to Turkey took place while Turkish officials carried out four presidential level, six prime ministerial level and six foreign ministerial level visits to Russia. In addition to these contacts at the state level, informal ties at economic and people-to-people levels gained momentum as well. Turkish and Russian business people frequently came together in gatherings held by Turkish and Russian business associations and economic cooperation organizations. Russian tourists selecting Turkey for their vacations rose continuously between the years 2000 and 2014 recording a nearly sixfold increase in figures in 14 years. Educational and social links between the two countries strengthened as well through marriages and student exchanges. Moreover, there was also progress in cooperation between Turkey and Russia in academic and intellectual level. Turkish and Russian academics, journalists and field specialists occasionally came together in conferences, workshops, round-table meetings and discussed the current state and future of the relationship.

There was absence of hierarchy related to issues. Economic matters had gained as much weight and eminence in the Turkish–Russian relationship as the political and security matters. Topics concerning trade, energy cooperation, strengthening of bilateral economic ties were discussed thoroughly along with security problems in the Middle East and North Africa and possible areas of collaboration in the Black Sea and the South Caucasus regions in the annual High-Level Russian–Turkish Cooperation Council meetings between the two countries (President of Russia 2011, 2013, 2014). Turkey strove to reduce its trade deficit to Russia resulting from large amounts of natural gas purchases at high prices from this country by augmenting the number and diversity of Turkish investments in Russia. Russia, on the other hand, speeded up its policy of laying its capital in different sectors of the Turkish economy in the form of acquisitions and joint ventures. In this regard, Moscow invested in strategic sectors of the Turkish economy such as banking, energy, technology and heavy industry.

Turkey and Russia had different (in fact, in some cases opposite) views with regard to some bilateral and regional matters on security and politics, but nevertheless they were able to utilize bargaining, negotiation and consensus-building tools rather than military instruments while seeking a way out of these issues until the November 2015 crisis.

Russia became the first state to recognize the independence and sovereignty of the breakaway regions of Abkhazia and South Ossetia when they declared their liberty from Georgia, whereas Turkey supported the sanctity of the borders and territorial integrity of the Georgian state. The situation was reversed in the Balkans. Turkey was one of the earliest recognizers of independent Kosovo in contrast to Russia that respected the authority and jurisdiction of Serbia over that territory.

Turkey pursued a pro-Azerbaijani line pertaining to the Nagorno-Karabakh problem and opted for a resolution that would reinstate jurisdiction of Baku in the disputed territory and made this the primary precondition of a possible reconciliation with Armenia. Russia, on the other hand, declared that it was following an impartial course by being in an equidistant position of both sides of the conflict. Yet, Moscow's past pro-Armenian record regarding the issue, coupled with its being Yerevan's chief arm, military supplier and credit supplier, eroded the veracity of this claim.

Turkey and Russia gave different reactions to the referendum held in Crimea on March 16, 2014 as well which resulted in triumph of the option of integration of the region into Russia over the choice of preservation of the status of the peninsula as part of Ukraine. While Moscow rapidly and happily hailed the upshot of the referendum and signed the agreement that would cede Crimea to Russia on March 18, 2014, Ankara defined the referendum as unlawful and illegitimate and declared that Turkey would not recognize any decisions that would emanate from the outcome of the referendum (Republic of Turkey Ministry of Foreign Affairs 2014).

Lastly, although the two states did not see eye to eye in their most thorny and sensitive issue, namely the Chechen and the Kurdish separatism, and from time to time accused each other of condoning illegal and subversive activities of extremist and terrorist groups on their respective territories, they never came close to engaging in a military confrontation even for these serious and vital matters.

The internal conflict in Syria appeared to be another regional hotspot where views of Turkey and Russia diverged to a great extent. Turkey was opposed to any solution which would involve President Bashar al-Assad, who in Ankara's view, long time ago lost his legitimacy because of his harsh treatment of the opposition to his administration. Russia's peace plans to stop violence in Syria, on the other hand, included al-Assad, at least as a figure who would play a critical role in the political transition process in the war-torn country. The political disagreement over Syria, however, evolved into a minor military conflict after Turkey's downing of the Russian bomber and this development rapidly and sharply deteriorated all aspects of the bilateral relationship.

The third change in Turkish–Russian relations can be portrayed as a leader-driven change which resulted from decisions of authoritative policy-makers (C. Hermann 1990, 11), Erdoğan and Putin who had the determination, power and capacity to compel their respective governments to change course. So the next part of the study will briefly examine the current domestic political structure of Russia and Turkey and will evaluate the impact of two presidents on the course of the relationship.

Leadership theory

Both Russia and Turkey have been receding in terms of democratic credentials for quite some time (Diamond 2015, 145–6). Although Putin and Erdoğan won landslide victories by gaining 63.6 percent and 51.8 percent of the vote respectively in the presidential elections of March 2012 and August 2014, there were serious question marks regarding the fairness of these elections. In both of the election campaigns, Putin and Erdoğan as incumbent prime ministers were granted biased media coverage especially in public broadcasting channels to the detriment of other contestants (Organization for Security and Cooperation in Europe 2012, 1, 2014, 1–2). Furthermore, they benefited to a great extent from state resources such as government transport and staff during the campaigning period and used the state events as platforms to canvass for votes.

Russia and Turkey have been witnessing a roll-back of civil liberties under the rule of Putin and Erdoğan. The state-owned media outlets along with broadcasting channels owned by friendly businessmen serve as significant vehicles for supporting and disseminating pro-government propaganda and for labelling any kinds of opposition and criticism as acts which endanger national security. The few remaining representatives of independent media grapple with the intimidation effect (Hale, McFaul, and Colton 2004, 311) such as government pressure for firing of dissident journalists, harassment by tax authorities, lawsuits of defamation, extremism, terrorism and threat of closure. The restrictions on freedom of assembly have become evident as well. Russia imposed new fines on individuals participating in unauthorized gatherings and organizations that planned such meetings, and amended the NGO law in July 2012 to oblige all NGOs involved in political activity and receiving foreign funding to be registered as foreign agents (Lanskoy and Suthers 2013, 78–80). Erdoğan, on the other hand, approved a new legislation in May 2015 which increased criminal punishment for various actions during protests and permitted police to open fire on demonstrators who used incendiaries (Freedom House 2016a).

The independence and impartiality of the judiciary has been undermined to a large extent both in Russia and Turkey. The executive branch has become quite decisive and influential in career advancement and compensation of judiciary personnel, which has cast a long shadow on the decisions of the courts in controversial cases (Freedom House 2016b). The emergence of a dependent and obedient judiciary gave rise to the erosion of the rule of law and separation of powers, thus weakening horizontal accountability in both of the countries.

Russia and Turkey have witnessed throughout the years concentration and consolidation of power in the hands of assertive, charismatic and populist leaders who held sway over significant domestic and foreign policy matters. Foreign policy is made and carried out by a single group in both states which is composed of the president, prime minister, foreign and defense ministers and trusted advisers and bureaucrats. The group is small, is made up of loyal members and power is skewed in favor of the president. Due to the unequal power configuration within the group, members seek concurrence to minimize conflict, retain their position and sustain cohesiveness of the group. Therefore, decisions made with concurrence might result in conflictual behavior which utilizes military and economic sanctions rather than instruments of diplomacy as the participants are assured of others' support (M. Hermann 2001, 70).

Erdoğan and Putin, leaders with high need for power, belief in ability to control events coupled with strong distrust of others (Görener and Ucal 2011, 367–8; Egorova and Egorova 2016), exert considerable influence on foreign policy decisions by taking advantage of their dominant position in the single group. They are ready to act quickly and decisively to confront any challenges to their authority. So, Erdoğan might have wanted to teach Putin a lesson for repeated violations of Turkey's airspace and Russian bombardment of combat groups close to Turkey, whereas Putin who strove hard to enhance Russia's global status and prestige regarded the downing of the Russian bomber by Turkey as a personal insult and responded to this perceived unfriendly and disrespectful act with harsh economic measures.

The crisis of November 2015 revealed that the two leaders who had made significant contributions to the development of bilateral ties between Turkey and Russia had the potential to undercut the burgeoning relationship. Yet, the fact that Erdoğan decided to back off from his hard-hitting policy line after a while and took the step to normalize Turkish–Russian relations, and Putin's positive reaction to this move, manifested that political, economic and people-to-people ties built over the years between the two states were deemed too valuable to forgo easily.

It seems that increasing economic cooperation along with growing political interaction did not suffice to create the conditions of political integration between Turkey and Russia as the complex interdependency theory foresaw. This could be attributed to the absence of common institutions in regions of common interest such as South Caucasus, Central Asia and the Middle East which could act as mechanisms to defuse prospective crises and ensure policy coordination. The Black Sea Economic Cooperation (BSEC) could be taken as a good example in this context. The BSEC has been serving as the common institution between Turkey and Russia since the end of the Cold War and there exists considerable policy harmonization between the two states with regard to Black Sea matters. The organization, despite its drawbacks, proved to be quite instrumental in straightening out kinks between Ankara and Moscow regarding Black Sea issues and to set forth joint security structures. The foundation of similar organizations, especially in crisis-prone regions of South Caucasus and the Middle East, might be the key to assure enduring reconciliation between Turkey and Russia.

Research design

I used two data-collection methods in this book: analysis of documents concerning the topic under investigation along with the conduct of in-depth interviews with people who were equipped with relevant knowledge and experience about the subject under study and also had access to insider information.

The main limitation of this study is the author's lack of proficiency in the Russian language. In order to compensate for this shortfall, I resorted extensively to Russian primary and secondary sources written in English and Turkish. Within this framework, websites of the Russian presidency, Government of the Russian Federation and Ministry of Foreign Affairs of Russia were quite helpful as they included English versions of speeches, statements, news conferences, ratifications, official meetings, press releases of Russian foreign policy-makers as well as basic documents on Russian foreign policy. The web page of the Embassy of the Russian Federation in Turkey was also useful as it encapsulated valuable information about the political agreements between Turkey and Russia along with meetings that took place between the high-level officials of two countries. I also made use of books and articles in academic journals written by Russian academics, field specialists and journalists as secondary sources in order to provide comprehensive, accurate, and insightful account of the Russian side. Furthermore, I utilized to a great extent the websites of Turkish Ministry of Foreign Affairs, Turkish Official Gazette and State Planning Organization as they included official documents in the form of agreements, memorandums of understanding, protocols and joint declarations, press releases and statements.

The elite interviews I carried out with the representatives of the Turkish–Russian business associations and the officials in the Turkish Foreign Ministry who were specialized in Turkish–Russian political and commercial affairs constituted my other primary sources in this research. These interviews were in-depth one-on-one conversations during which I posed a couple of open-ended questions to the interviewees to draw out their views and opinions pertaining to the Turkish–Russian relations. Interviews with these people were helpful in the sense that they provided up-to-date information with regard to the state of Turkish–Russian interaction, brought out new insights into the topics under study and corroborated my preliminary analyses and findings concerning the nature of the political and economic relations between the two states. When it was not possible to conduct face-to-face interviews due to the participants' remote locations, as was the case with officials that were serving at the Moscow Embassy of Turkey, telephone interviews and email correspondence were used in order to compensate for this shortcoming.

I also attempted to conduct interviews with the Russian diplomats and business people with the aim of getting first-hand information about the Russian ideas, views and projections concerning the current outlook and future status of the Turkish–Russian relations, but unfortunately failed at the endeavor despite many attempts in this direction and this is another caveat of this research.

Secondary sources such as statistical data from the Turkish Institute of Statistics, Russian Federation Federal State Statistics Service, Petroleum Pipeline Company (BOTAŞ), Energy Market Regulatory Authority (EPDK), Central Bank of Turkey, Turkish Ministry of Tourism and Culture, and Office of the Commercial Counsellor of Turkish Embassy in Moscow, websites of the Turkish armed forces and Undersecretariat for Defense Industries, reports prepared by trade organizations and business councils, papers of international organizations and newspaper and news agency archives were widely used throughout this book in order to gather data.

Organization of the study

This book is composed in three parts organized to examine the basic parameters of post-Cold War Turkish–Russian relations. Part I starts with throwing light on the foundation of a multifaceted relationship between Turkey and Russia in the wake of the Cold War through strengthening political dialogue between the two countries as a result of signing political agreements towards this end and creating mechanisms for diplomatic collaboration. This part also deals with the emergence and growing prominence of business interest groups which strive for the advancement of political and economic relations between the two states to ensure less problematic business environment for themselves along with deepening and expansion of social ties between the peoples of Russia and Turkey via marriages, student and touristic exchanges and academic interaction. This section ends with the investigation of the weakest link between Turkey and Russia: security ties.

Part II of the book delves into the issues of cooperation and competition between Turkey and Russia in South Caucasus, Central Asia, Black Sea and Middle East regions in addition to the impact of the separatist Chechen and Kurdish currents on the bilateral relationship in five chapters. The views of Turkey and Russia converged at most in the Black Sea; the rivalry between them took an increasingly economic form in Central Asia, while the main points of divergence and friction became the Nagorno-Karabakh and Syria matters as the two countries extended their political, economic and military support to the opposite sides in these conflicts. The issue of ethnic separatism, a long-term difficult and scathing internal problem for both Turkey and Russia retains the potential to impinge on the relationship as well especially in the wake of developments in Syria.

The post-Cold War era witnessed salient augmentation, institutionalization and diversification of economic and commercial bonds between Turkey and Russia. Although they have not yet reached to the maturity level to hinder the rupture in the relationship caused by disagreement over a political matter, they have nevertheless been influential to urge Ankara and Moscow to put the relationship back on track. Therefore, Part III of the study is devoted to the detailed examination of the growing cooperation between Russia and Turkey in the post-Cold War years in the fields of bilateral trade, energy, construction and contracting services and investments.

References

Agg, Catherine. 2006. "Trends in Government Support for Non-Governmental Organizations: Is the 'Golden Age' of the NGO behind Us?" *United Nations Research Institute for Social Development Civil Society and Social Movements Programme Paper*, no. 23: 1–30.

Diamond, Larry. 2015. "Facing Up to the Democratic Recession." *Journal of Democracy* 26(1): 141–155.

Egorova, Ekaterina, and Elizaveta Egorova. 2016. "Erdoğan and Putin: The Game of Thrones." *Radnor Reports*, April 6.
Freedom House. 2016a. *Freedom in the World 2016 Report: Turkey*. Freedom House. Accessed July 8, 2016. https://freedomhouse.org/report/freedom-world/2016/turkey/.
Freedom House. 2016b. *Freedom in the World 2016 Report: Russia*. Freedom House. Accessed July 8, 2016. https://freedomhouse.org/report/freedom-world/2016/russia/.
Görener, Aylin Ş., and Meltem Ş. Ucal. 2011. "The Personality and Leadership Style of Recep Tayyip Erdoğan: Implications for Turkish Foreign Policy." *Turkish Studies* 12(3): 357–381.
Hale, Henry E., Michael McFaul, and Timothy J. Colton. 2004. "Putin and the 'Delegative Democracy' Trap: Evidence from Russia's 2003–2004 Elections." *Post-Soviet Affairs* 20(4): 285–319.
Hermann, Charles F. 1990. "Changing Course: When Governments Choose to Redirect Foreign Policy." *International Studies Quarterly* 34(1): 3–21.
Hermann, Margaret G. 2001. "How Decision Units Shape Foreign Policy: A Theoretical Framework." *International Studies Review* 3(2): 47–81.
Keohane, Robert O. 1993. "Institutional Theory and the Realist Challenge after the Cold War." In *Neorealism and Neoliberalism: The Contemporary Debate*, edited by David A. Baldwin, 269–300. New York: Columbia University Press.
Keohane, Robert O., and Joseph S. Nye Jr. 1977. *Power and Interdependence: World Politics in Transition*. Boston: Little Brown.
Keohane, Robert O., and Joseph S. Nye Jr. 2000. "Globalization: What's New? What's Not? (And So What?)" *Foreign Policy*, 118: 104–119.
Lanskoy, Miriam, and Elspeth Suthers. 2013. "Outlawing the Opposition." *Journal of Democracy* 24(3): 75–87.
Milner, Helen V. 2009. "Power, Interdependence, and Nonstate Actors in World Politics: Research Frontiers." In *Power, Interdependence, and Nonstate Actors in World Politics*, edited by Helen V. Milner and Andrew Moravcsik, 3–27. Princeton: Princeton University Press.
Organization for Security and Cooperation in Europe. 2012. *Russian Federation: Presidential Election 4 March 2012*. Warsaw: OSCE/ODIHR.
Organization for Security and Cooperation in Europe. 2014. *Republic of Turkey: Presidential Election 10 August 2014*. Warsaw: OSCE/ODIHR.
President of Russia. 2011. "Meeting of High-Level Russian-Turkish Cooperation Council." Accessed January 8, 2015. http://eng.kremlin.ru/transcripts/1917/.
President of Russia. 2013. "Meeting of High-Level Russian-Turkish Cooperation Council." Accessed January 8, 2015. http://eng.kremlin.ru/news/6316/.
President of Russia. 2014. "Meeting of High-Level Russian-Turkish Cooperation Council." Accessed January 8, 2015. http://eng.kremlin.ru/news/23321/.

President of Russia. 2016. "Vladimir Putin Received a Letter from President of Turkey Recep Tayyip Erdogan." *President of Russia*. Accessed June 28, 2016. http://en.kremlin.ru/events/president/news/52282/.

Republic of Turkey Ministry of Foreign Affairs. 2014. "Press Release Regarding the Referendum Held in Crimea." *Republic of Turkey Ministry of Foreign Affairs*. Accessed January 8, 2015. http://www.mfa.gov.tr/no_-86_-17-march-2014_-press-release-regarding-the-referendum-held-in-crimea.en.mfa/.

RT, "Turkey Says Su-34 Violated Airspace, Moscow Shrugs off Report as 'Propaganda.'" 2016. January 30.

United Nations Conference on Trade and Development. 2009. *World Investment Report: Transnational Corporations, Agricultural Production and Development. United Nations Conference on Trade and Development*. Accessed January 3, 2015. http://unctad.org/en/docs/wir2009_en.pdf/.

United Nations General Assembly. 2015. Regular Sessions. *United Nations*. Accessed January 4, 2015. http://research.un.org/en/docs/ga/quick/regular/68/.

Part I
Multiple ties that bind Turkey and Russia

1 Flourishing of a multifaceted relationship

The first proposition of the complex interdependency theory points out the emergence of a more entwined and integrated international system owing to the developments in transportation, communication and technology in which there exist various points of contact between the countries at both official and public levels. Official relations are conducted by politicians and bureaucrats in meetings, on the telephone and in official correspondence (Keohane and Nye 1977, 26). Transnational ties, on the other hand, have gained remarkable prominence especially with growing power and expansion of business along with increased people-to-people exchanges between the ordinary citizens which brought about a blurring of the lines between domestic and foreign policy and added more items on the agenda of foreign policy officials.

The years following the end of the Cold War have witnessed intensification and deepening of Turkish–Russian interaction on many platforms in accordance with the first premise of the complex interdependency theory. While high-level political exchanges formed the basis and the agreements signed at the end of these meetings set guidelines for future progress of the relationship, increasing activism of business interest groups along with growing people-to-people contacts through tourism, marriage, education and academic exchange further strengthened the bilateral ties between the two countries. Some progress has been recorded even in military relations that barely existed 25 years ago.

The erosion of political relations between Turkey and Russia following the plane crisis took its toll in other aspects of the relationship as well. Yet, grievances stemmed from losing important business and people-to-people connections led the non-state actors on both sides to mediate between the two leaders to reinitiate the political dialogue between the two countries. The active role played by Turkish and

Russian businessmen in reopening the channels of communication between Erdoğan and Putin (Yetkin 2016) demonstrated once more the importance of the presence of multiple ties between Turkey and Russia in keeping the relationship on track. This chapter will examine these various ties that connect Turkey and Russia which have played crucial role both in the foundation and perpetuation of a multifaceted relationship between the two states in the post-Cold War era.

Growing and deepening political dialogue

The Treaty on the Principles of Relations between Russia and Turkey that was signed on May 25, 1992 during Turkish Prime Minister Süleyman Demirel's official visit to Moscow became the first blueprint that determined the basic contours of Turkish–Russian relations in the post-Cold War era. As per the agreement, the two parties pledged to develop their relations within the framework of respect for political independence, sovereignty and territorial integrity, non-interference in domestic affairs, equality of rights and mutual interests (Republic of Turkey Ministry of Foreign Affairs 1992).

Despite expressions of good intentions and statements of good will, rivalry in the South Caucasus, Central Asia and Balkans, coupled with mutual complaints of supporting the separatist currents in each other's soil hampered the advancement of bilateral relations in the immediate post-Cold War period. The watershed which would engender a marked rapprochement between the two countries came in 1997 when the Russian Prime Minister Viktor Chernomyrdin visited Turkey on December 15–17 and signed with his Turkish counterpart Mesut Yılmaz the Blue Stream gas agreement that would strengthen the energy partnership between the two states. In addition to the natural gas accord, agreements regarding cooperation in customs matters, prevention of double taxation and reciprocal encouragement and protection of investments were also concluded in order to facilitate the activities of Turkish and Russian businessmen. Following the signatures, while Chernomyrdin stated that Russia and Turkey should leave behind the Chechen and Kurdish issues and concentrate on the establishment of powerful economic ties which would contribute to the normalization of political relations between the two countries, Yılmaz declared that Turkey desired to cooperate rather than compete with its great neighbor (*Ayın Tarihi*, December 15, 1997).

The agreements with Russia had come at a time when Turkey was facing difficulties in its relations with the EU and the Middle Eastern countries. A few days before Chernomyrdin's visit, Turkey was denied candidate status at the EU Luxembourg summit and the Turkish President Demirel was criticized heavily by many Arab countries at the Organization of Islamic Conference summit in Tehran because of Turkey's defense agreement with Israel and military operations in the north of Iraq. The thaw with Russia owing to these circumstances was considered significant and valuable for Turkish officials at least to demonstrate that Turkey was not devoid of prospective allies in its neighborhood.

The disruptive economic crises erupted in Russia in 1998 and in Turkey in 2001 contributed to a great extent to the Turkish–Russian reconciliation. With a run-down economy that was in urgent need of cash, Russia started to see Turkey not just as a relentless competitor that continuously strove to curb the Russian influence in the South Caucasus and Central Asia but also as a potential client of its rich natural gas resources. Compromise and accommodation in its intricate relationship with Russia was also appealing to Turkey as large Russian market could cure some of the ills of the severe financial crisis that had hit most of the Turkish companies. So, despite the ongoing rivalry in the South Caucasus and Central Asia and the existence of different point of views pertaining to some regional affairs such as the Kosovo War, elevating economic relations crowned by the construction of Blue Stream gas pipeline project led to a rapprochement in political matters which resulted in the signing of the Action Plan for Cooperation in Eurasia: From Bilateral Cooperation towards Multi-dimensional Partnership by Turkish Foreign Minister İsmail Cem and his Russian counterpart Igor Ivanov on November 16, 2001. The document envisaged common foreign policy outlook and joint course of action on behalf of Turkey and Russia for the creation of conditions for peace, stability and welfare in a vast area encompassing the Balkan, Black Sea, South Caucasus, Central Asia and Middle East regions. With the Action Plan, the two countries also decided to establish the Joint Working Group which would be made up of the representatives of the ministries of foreign affairs and where prospects for improvement of relations on a bilateral basis and in the Eurasian platform would be taken up (Embassy of the Russian Federation in Turkey 2001). This mechanism, while increasing the number of direct contacts between the officials of Russia and Turkey, would also facilitate the implementation of concrete measures in various areas of relations.

Turkish–Russian relations elevated into a new dimension with Putin's consolidation of authority in Russia and Justice and Development Party (AKP)'s coming to power in Turkey at the beginning of 2000s. Two important documents, Joint Declaration on Deepening of

Friendship and Multi-dimensional Partnership of 2004 and Joint Declaration on Progress towards a New Stage in Relations and Further Deepening of Friendship and Multi-dimensional Partnership of 2009 were signed, both of which underlined that the two states had close or similar positions with regard to many regional and international matters and their collaboration in Eurasia would contribute to the security, stability and welfare in the region (Embassy of the Russian Federation in Turkey 2004; Republic of Turkey Ministry of Foreign Affairs 2009).

Significant steps towards the institutionalization of the relationship have been taken in the recent years. The High-Level Cooperation Council, a mechanism that would act as the guiding body in setting the strategy and main directions for developing Russian–Turkish relations, was established in May 2010 in the course of Russian President Dmitry Medvedev's visit to Turkey. The Council would meet annually and coordinate implementation of important political, trade and economic projects as well as facilitation of cultural and humanitarian cooperation (President of Russia 2010). A public forum that would be composed of famous and reputable figures of Turkey and Russia was also established within the capacity of the Council in order to bring Turkish and Russian nations closer (Yağmur Güldere, Undersecretary of the Moscow Embassy of the Republic of Turkey, email correspondence with the author, October 27, 2010).

Reciprocal formal visits at the presidential, premier, ministerial levels, contacts between the friendship groups, functional committees and expert commissions of two parliaments, regular meetings and consultations held between the state agencies along with the formation of cooperation mechanisms strengthened the foundations of the Turkish–Russian relations and earned them a solid and institutional character in the post-Cold War period. Even so, development of amicable political ties between the lower echelons of Turkish and Russian establishment is very much dependent on good rapport at the top level. This situation was confirmed after Russian Federation Council speaker Valentina Matviyenko stated on June 29, 2016, right after the thaw between Erdoğan and Putin, that they were ready to resume inter-parliamentary relations with the Turkish Parliament which had been frozen in December 2015 after the plane incident ("Russian Upper House" 2016).

Increasing visibility and influence of the business community

The economic relations between Turkey and Russia recorded an impressive progress in the immediate post-Cold War period despite tensions in the political atmosphere. The removal of travel restrictions, along with rise of unemployment in Russia as a result of limited job opportunities in the nascent private sector of the country in the post-Soviet period led some Russian citizens to engage in suitcase trade in Turkey, which as a result of liberalization measures taken at the beginning of 1980s, had transformed its economy based on import-substitution to an export-oriented one and had earned a good reputation for manufacturing of textile and consumer products. Turkey's geographical proximity to Russia, the low price of the Turkish goods compared to their equivalents in the Western markets, and the Turkish government's decision to ease visa requirements first for the citizens of the Soviet Union then for the nationals of the successor states made Turkey an attractive destination for Russian suitcase traders. Some of these people also started to visit Turkey as tourists in the ensuing years or recommended their fellow citizens to choose Turkey for their vacations which contributed positively to the developing of social bonds between the two societies whose interaction had been until that period was very limited due to the Cold War conditions.

This was also an era when Turkish companies started to invest in the Russian economy especially in banking, construction, retail and consumer goods sectors and reaped benefits of low competition there when most of the Western businesses stayed away from the Russian market as they did not want to deal with the travails of a transition economy. These early pioneers opened the way for other Turkish entrepreneurs in Russia and they, together with the suitcase traders, acquainted the citizens of Russia with Turkish goods and services.

This period also witnessed the emergence and growing prominence of Turkish business interest groups such as Turkish–Russian Business Council, Laleli Industrialists and Businessmen Association, Merter Industrialists and Businessmen Association, Russian–Turkish Businessmen Association and Russian-Turkish Business and Friendship Association, whose members were composed of people doing business in Russia or with Russian citizens. These organizations entered into contact with government officials occasionally, conveyed their demands, suggestions as well as grievances regarding Turkish–Russian economic interaction, and commenced to act as important lobbying mechanisms for development of better political relations between Turkey and Russia (Şaban Gül, Project Manager, Russian-Turkish Business and Friendship Association, interview with the author, February 25, 2008). These increasing contacts at the business level as well as growing bilateral trade forced Turkey and Russia to prepare the legal framework for the further development of the economic relations between the two countries. Agreements signed in 1997 regarding customs matters, prevention of double taxation and promotion of reciprocal investments should be taken in this sense. Furthermore, lobbying activities of some of the Turkish construction firms that did business in Russia were influential in realization of the Blue Stream gas pipeline project which became the major mortar that glued the future of the two countries.

The growing and diversifying economic relations especially in the fields of energy, construction, fast-moving consumer goods and manufacturing sectors, along with increasing mutual investments created a strong and lasting foundation for political association between Turkey and Russia throughout the years. The activities and initiatives of Turkish professional business organizations such as Antalya Fruit and Vegetable Exporters Union, Turkish Exporters Assembly and International Transporters Association should also be mentioned here as, whenever Turkish companies encountered difficulties in their interaction with the Russian authorities, they actively stepped in and struggled to solve the problem by bringing forth new policy options and engaging Turkish officials as well as government members for the resolution of the conflict.

Developing and diversifying people-to-people ties

Mixed marriages, student exchanges, tourist visits and academic interaction all have had a positive impact on consolidation of social and cultural bonds between Turkey and Russia in the post-Cold War period. Three hundred thousand marriages between Turkish and Russian citizens occurred ("300,000 Marriages" 2012) and 1 million children born out of these marriages will act as a cultural bridge between the two nations in the coming years. Education, culture, friendship associations founded in the cities of İstanbul, Ankara, İzmir, Antalya and St. Petersburg by Turkish and Russian citizens also contributed to the development of social and cultural ties between the two societies through opening of Turkish and Russian language courses, organizing exhibitions, arranging tourist visits to Turkey and Russia, holding conferences and extending help in legal matters.

There have been approximately 1,100 Turkish students (Embassy of the Republic of Turkey in Moscow 2016) studying in higher education institutions in Russia, about 300 of whom specialize on nuclear technology, whereas 1,157 Russian students have been studying in Turkish universities, according to 2015 figures (Higher Education Council 2015). Some of the Turkish university students receiving education in the cities of Obninsk, Voronezh and Saratov were reported to have been expelled from their institutions following the rift between Turkey and Russia (Dolgov 2015). Russia acknowledged the expulsion of eight Turkish students from the Voronezh Institute of High Technologies but maintained that they were dismissed because of academic failure and poor attendance rather than for political reasons (Ministry of Foreign Affairs of the Russian Federation 2015).

Tourism is another burgeoning area for Turkish–Russian interaction. Russian tourists started visiting Turkey in the early 1990s after Turkey eased its visa requirements for citizens of the successor states of the Soviet Union.[1] Their numbers increased consistently throughout the years and by sending nearly four and a half million tourists to Turkey in 2014, Russia came second after Germany in terms of the total number of tourists traveling to Turkey. Most Russian tourists prefer Aegean and Mediterranean sunspots such as Antalya, Dalaman, Bodrum, Fethiye, Kuşadası for their vacations, whereas the number of those choosing mountain resorts such as Uludağ and Palandöken as well as İstanbul and the cities of Black Sea region has also scaled up steadily over the years.

The seven-month crisis between Turkey and Russia has been a hard time both for Russian tourists planning to visit Turkey and for their Turkish hosts. Three days after the plane incident Putin signed an executive order that suspended sales of tours to Turkey and introduced a ban on charter flights between the two countries (President of Russia 2016). These measures engendered a sharp decline in number of the Russian tourists to Turkey. While 801,915 Russians came to Turkey between January and May 2015, the figure dropped to 138,181 one year later, recording an 83 percent decrease (Republic of Turkey Ministry of Culture and Tourism 2016). This was a lose-lose situation for both Turkish and Russian people. While hotels were closed down in tourist resorts in Turkey and many Turkish people lost their jobs, Russian tourists were deprived of a holiday destination which was geographically close to Russia, offered high-quality and affordable service and applied a visa-free regime. Therefore, Putin's amendments to the November executive order on June 30, 2016 which repealed former restrictions were received happily both by Turkish hoteliers and Russian travelers and the first Russian organized group of 189 tourists that landed at Antalya airport on July 9, 2016 was welcomed with flowers ("İlk Rus" 2016).

At the academic and intellectual level Turkish think tanks and research centers such as ORSAM, TEPAV, SETA and Turkish Historical Society (TTK), along with their Russian counterparts, namely

RISS, IVRAN and Valdai Club, started to organize joint conferences, workshops and round-table meetings on a regular basis in which historians, international relations scholars, journalists, field specialists, opinion leaders, businessmen and former politicians from Turkey and Russia came together to discuss background, current dynamics and future orientation of Turkish–Russian relations and evaluated possible areas of cooperation between the two countries in the South Caucasus, Central Asia and Middle East regions.

There existed also a small group of Turkish and Russian intellectuals called Neo-Eurasianists who suggested closer and deeper Turkish–Russian collaboration, in the form of Eurasian Union, which might also brace other regional powers such as Iran and China and would act as a balancing force against the EU and United States of America (USA) in international politics (Gürkan 2001, 70). This movement was composed of Turkish and Russian politicians, journalists, writers, academics and former military officers who belonged to different political factions. What brought them together was their deep uneasiness and suspicion regarding Western policies in the regions surrounding Turkey and Russia. The Turkish Eurasianists stood against the American policies in the Middle East firmly, objected specifically to the invasion of Iraq, and Washington's close association with the Kurds of Iraq, fearing that these developments would arouse separatist sentiments among the Kurdish population in Turkey and undermine the unity and territorial integrity of the Turkish state. They also fervently opposed the EU, especially with regard to the Cyprus issue and stated that the EU pursued pro-Greek and Greek-Cypriot policies at the expense of the interests of Turkey and the Turkish-Cypriot people. The Russian Eurasianists, on the other hand, were equally uncomfortable with the American operations in Iraq and were also annoyed with the color revolutions that took place in Georgia, Ukraine and Kyrgyzstan which in their view would serve to curb the Russian influence in its near abroad (Berman 2005). Although Turkish and Russian Eurasianists favored and promoted closer Turkish–Russian interaction, their contribution to Turkish–Russian rapprochement had been marginal compared to the impact of business interest groups due to the fact that their access to decision-making structures in their respective countries was limited.

Foundation of military relations

Military relations had been the weakest link between the Soviet Union and Turkey during the Cold War years because the former, being the leader of a security bloc (the Warsaw Pact), which had been set up to counteract the activities of North Atlantic Treaty Organization (NATO), the rival defense organization of which Turkey had been one of the leading members. However, with the end of the Cold War and the dissolution of the Warsaw Pact, it also became necessary to rethink and redefine the military aspect of the relationship. Military relations between Russia and Turkey began with the signing of the Memorandum of Understanding by the Ministries of Defense of the two countries on May 11, 1993. This was followed by the Agreement on Turkey's Purchases of Military Equipment from the Russian Federation that was concluded on October 31, 1993. With the latter accord Turkey purchased 19 general purpose Mi-17V (Hip H) helicopters, 70 BTR-80 armoured personnel carriers and other weapons worth a total of 114 million dollars (Kandaurov 2013). The arms contract with Russia was significant for Turkey due to two reasons. First, it became the first NATO country to buy arms and military equipment from Russia. Second, the deal came at a time when Turkey's Western allies refused to sell military hardware to Turkey on the grounds of violation of the human rights by Turkish armed forces in their struggle against Kurdistan Workers' Party (PKK).

The Turkish Minister of National Defense Mehmet Gölhan and the Russian Minister of Defense General Pavel Grachev concluded the Agreement on Cooperation in Military Technical Matters and in the Field of Defense Industry on April 20, 1994 which aimed to extend collaboration in the sectors of development, production and supply of defense goods and services between the two countries through joint programmes, projects and the exchange of technical information (Republic of Turkey Ministry of Foreign Affairs 1994). The accord also envisaged the establishment of a joint committee for the implementation of the clauses of the agreement which was realized on May 16, 2002.

Collaboration in the military sphere between Turkey and Russia remained at modest levels compared to political, economic and social realms mostly as a result of hesitation and restraint on the Turkish side resulting from its membership of NATO. Therefore, it is not surprising that military and technical cooperation with Ankara is under 1 percent of Rosoboronexport's, Russian state defense products procurement company, turnover (Litovkin 2013). Nevertheless, some kind of progress has been recorded. Turkey signed an agreement with Rosoboronexport on August 29, 2008 to purchase medium-range anti-tank weapon systems that involved 80 weapon units and 800 missiles. With the deal, the Russian arms-industry managed to re-enter the Turkish market after a 15-year hiatus by beating its American and Israeli competitors (Undersecretariat for Defense Industries 2008).

Russia also participated to Turkey's attack helicopter bid with its Kamov Ka-50-2 Erdoğan type helicopters. Although the Russian side was one of the two shortlisters in the competition, the bid was cancelled in May 2004 much to the dismay and disappointment of Moscow. The negative impact of Turkey's experience with Mi-17V helicopters was an important obstacle that stood in the way of Russia, as 2 of the 19 helicopters Turkey bought from the country in 1993 crashed, 13 of them were put in warehouses due to mechanical malfunction and the remaining 4 helicopters that were sent to Russia in 2003 for maintenance had not been sent back.[2]

The nascent military relations between Turkey and Russia got their share from the Turkish–Russian dispute and were suspended following the November 2015 crisis. This was bad news for the Turkish defense industry as the Turkish and Russian military specialists were working jointly on the design and manufacturing of a short-range air defense system before the rift (Akulov 2016). The revitalization of the security ties between Ankara and Moscow will probably take some time and a possible thaw in this aspect of the association seems to be contingent upon convergence of Turkish and Russian positions pertaining to Syria.

The last two decades have witnessed the emergence of multiple ties that bind Turkey and Russia. Formal relations conducted at the interstate level form the crux of the Turkish–Russian interaction. Politicians from both sides had the will and determination to improve and institutionalize political bonds and so took necessary steps in this direction through signing official documents and establishing mechanisms which would contribute to the enhancement of cooperation and consultation between the different state organs of their respective countries. Yet, business-to-business and people-to-people ties proved to be equally valuable, as they acted as transmission belts at the time of political disagreements between Turkey and Russia by urging and motivating governmental elites to re-open channels of communication and to take measures to put the relationship back on track. Part II will elaborate the issues of competition and cooperation between Turkey and Russia in the post-Cold War period regarding common regions of interest and will probe the impact of interaction at several levels on the course of the relationship.

Notes

1 Putin was one of these early Russian tourists that visited Turkey. Years later in 2004, he would recall his first-hand experience in a press conference and would praise the Turkish visa system to a Greek journalist. See "Press Conference by President Vladimir Putin", The Ministry of Foreign Affairs of the Russian Federation, accessed February 16, 2013, http://www.mid.ru/bdomp/brp_4.nsf/f68cd37b84711611c3256f6d00541094/4fb0f1f9c0d53683c3256f740024dec4!OpenDocument/.
2 The missing four-helicopters issue was resolved in August 2011 in the wake of Erdoğan's visit to Moscow in March 2011 and his bringing up the issue with Putin. See Yahya Bostan, "Rusya Kayıp Helikopterleri Gönderdi", *Sabah*, August 12, 2011.

References

Akulov, Andrei. 2016. "Turkey Missed Great Chance to Modernize its Military." *Strategic Culture*, March 3.
Berman, Ilan. 2005. "Ideologue of Empire." *The Wall Street Journal*, November 3.
Dolgov, Anna. 2015. "Russian Engineering University Expels Turkish Students." *The Moscow Times*, December 11.
Dünya, 2012. "300,000 Marriages Made between Russian and Turkish People in 16 Years." December 4.
Embassy of the Republic of Turkey in Moscow. 2016. "Türkiye-Rusya Federasyonu Eğitim İlişkileri." *Embassy of the Republic of Turkey in Moscow*. Accessed July 12, 2016. http://moskova.be.mfa.gov.tr/ShowInfoNotes.aspx?ID=219908/.
Embassy of the Russian Federation in Turkey. 2001. "Rusya Federasyonu ile Türkiye Cumhuriyeti Arasında Avrasya'da İşbirliği Eylem Planı: İkili İşbirliğinden Çok Boyutlu Ortaklığa." *Embassy of the Russian Federation in Turkey*. Accessed February 10, 2013. http://www.turkey.mid.ru/relat_2_t.html/.
Embassy of the Russian Federation in Turkey. 2004. "Rusya Federasyonu ile Türkiye Cumhuriyeti Arasında Dostluğun ve Çok Boyutlu Ortaklığın Derinleştirilmesine İlişkin Ortak Deklarasyon." *Embassy of the Russian Federation in Turkey*. Accessed February 10, 2013. http://www.turkey.mid.ru/text_t73.html/.
Gürkan, İhsan. 2001. "Eurasia: The New Great Game and Turkey." In *Turkish Views on Eurasia*, edited by İsmail Soysal and Sevsen Aslantepe, 11–80. İstanbul: ISIS.
Higher Education Council. 2015. "Uyruğa Göre Öğrenci Sayıları Raporu." *Higher Education Council*. Accessed July 12, 2016. https://istatistik.yok.gov.tr/.
Hürriyet, 2016. "İlk Rus Turist Kafilesi Antalya'da." July 9.

Kandaurov, Sergei. 2013. "Russian Arms Exports to Greece, Cyprus and Turkey." *Moscow Defense Brief.* Accessed August 5, 2013. http://mdb.cast.ru/mdb/2-2002/at/raegct/.

Keohane, Robert O., and Joseph S. Nye Jr. 1977. *Power and Interdependence: World Politics in Transition.* Boston: Little Brown.

Litovkin, Dmitry. 2013. "Russia to Arm Turkey with New Military Arsenal." *Russia beyond the Headlines,* May 20.

Ministry of Foreign Affairs of the Russian Federation. 2015. "Comment by the Information and Press Department on the Alleged Dismissal of Turkish Students from Russian Universities." *Ministry of Foreign Affairs of the Russian Federation.* Accessed July 12, 2016. http://www.mid.ru/en/foreign_policy/news/-/asset_publisher/cKNonkJE02Bw/content/id/1989711/.

President of Russia. 2010. "Russia and Turkey Have Established the High-Level Cooperation Council." *President of Russia.* Accessed February 10, 2013. http://eng.kremlin.ru/text/news/2010/05/226021.shtml/.

President of Russia. 2016. "Executive Order on Measures to Ensure Russia's National Security and Protection of Russian Citizens against Criminal and Other Illegal Acts and on the Application of Special Economic Measures against Turkey." *President of Russia.* Accessed July 12, 2016. http://en.kremlin.ru/acts/news/50805/.

Republic of Turkey Ministry of Culture and Tourism. 2016. "Number of Arriving-Departing Foreigners and Citizens." *Republic of Turkey Ministry of Culture and Tourism.* Accessed July 12, 2016. http://yigm.kulturturizm.gov.tr/TR,9854/sinir-giris-cikis-istatistikleri.html/.

Republic of Turkey Ministry of Foreign Affairs. 1992. "Türkiye Cumhuriyeti ile Rusya Federasyonu Arasındaki İlişkilerin Esasları Hakkında Antlaşma." *Republic of Turkey Ministry of Foreign Affairs.* Accessed February 9, 2013. http://ua.mfa.gov.tr/.

Republic of Turkey Ministry of Foreign Affairs. 1994. "Türkiye Cumhuriyeti Hükümeti ile Rusya Federasyonu Hükümeti Arasında Askeri Teknik Konular ve Savunma Sanayi Alanında İşbirliği Yapılmasına Dair Anlaşma." *Republic of Turkey Ministry of Foreign Affairs.* Accessed August 5, 2013. http://www.mfa.gov.tr/mfa_tr/PDF_Pool/showUAFile.aspx/.

Republic of Turkey Ministry of Foreign Affairs. 2009. "Joint Declaration on Progress towards a New Stage in Relations and Further Deepening of Friendship and Multidimensional Partnership." *Republic of Turkey Ministry of Foreign Affairs.* Accessed February 10, 2013. http://www.mfa.gov.tr/joint-declaration-between-the-republic-of-turkey-and-the-russian-federation-on-progress-towards-a-new-stage-in-relations-and-further-deepening-of-friendship-and-multidimensional-partnership_-moscow_-13-february-2009.en.mfa/.

TASS, "Russian Upper House Ready to Resume Dialogue with Turkey-Speaker." 2016. June 29.

Undersecretariat for Defense Industries. 2008. "Orta Menzilli Tanksavar Silah Sistemi Projesi." *Undersecretariat for Defense Industries.* Accessed August 5,

2013. http://www.ssm.gov.tr/tr/projeler/roketfuzemuhimmat/prjgrptanksavar/pages/omtashaziralim__k.aspx/.

Yetkin, Murat. 2016. "Bir İşadamı Devredeydi." *Hürriyet*, June 29.

Part II
The issues of competition and cooperation

The third premise of complex interdependency theory rules out the option of recourse to military force except for matters of survival in the case of eruption of conflicts between the states that are in a complex interdependent relationship. First of all, the use of force or threat of resort to military instruments has costly effects on the accomplishment of economic goals. Second, the destructiveness of nuclear weapons makes any attack against a nuclear power dangerous and difficult. Finally, popular opposition to prolonged military conflicts, especially in the Western democracies, decreases the probability of waging military campaigns in these countries (Keohane and Nye 1977, 28–9).

Multiple bonds at various levels in states where complex interdependency prevails induce the officials of these countries to step in whenever a disagreement breaks out and to put into action mechanisms of negotiation, consultation and bargaining to ensure the resolution of the conflict peacefully. Furthermore, as military security lost its primacy among other issue areas, militarily strong states eschew using their power in this domain to control outcomes on matters in which they are less strong (Keohane and Nye 1977, 30).

The post-Cold War era has witnessed the emergence of many issues of convergence and divergence between Turkey and Russia in areas of common interest to both of them; namely, the South Caucasus, Central Asia, Black Sea and the Middle East as well as the struggle with separatist currents in their territories. Although joint working groups had been inaugurated between Ankara and Moscow over the years to discuss and negotiate in order to alleviate tension and search for ways for compromise and conciliation concerning disputed matters, they proved ineffective in policy coordination and anticipation of prospective crises especially in the South Caucasus and Middle East. This part of the study, while examining the degree of cooperation and competition between Turkey and Russia in each issue area in five chapters, will also assess to what extent the multilayered nature of the relationship restrained the policies of Turkey and Russia vis-à-vis each other when they were embroiled in discord and rivalry in the post-Cold War period.

2 Clashing positions amidst attempts to gain ground in the South Caucasus

The disintegration of the Soviet Union gave rise to both relief and caution among decision-making circles in Ankara in the immediate post-Cold War period. On the one hand, Turkey ceased to share a land border with Russia, which was still a formidable actor with its powerful army and nuclear weapons. With the removal of the Soviet grip from the Balkans, South Caucasus and Central Asia, Turkey found the opportunity to permeate these regions through political, economic and cultural mediums. On the other hand, the end of the Soviet empire presaged the wane of Turkey's own strategic importance as the southern flank of NATO and gendarme of the West and raised questions about Turkey's value and belonging to the Western alliance.

Further developments vindicated the Turkish apprehension regarding its future with the Western world. The European Commission declared on December 20, 1989 that the European Community was not ready to start accession negotiations with Turkey due to the major changes the Community was undergoing resulting from the third enlargement wave and the entry into force of the Single Act (Republic of Turkey Ministry of Foreign Affairs 1989). Furthermore, Turkey's economic difficulties, its political disputes with Greece along with the situation in Cyprus were counted as major factors that made the commencement of accession negotiations less likely in the near future.

The negative opinion of the European Commission with regard to opening of the accession negotiations had come at a time when Turkey was suffering from serious domestic problems. The separatist Kurdish movement, religious tensions, rampant inflation and high unemployment were severe problems that the country had to endure. This internal and external environment urged the Turkish foreign policy-makers to search for a new role in the international arena which would restore the country's privileged position in the Cold War period and also allay its internal troubles.

The forging of close links with the states of South Caucasus and Central Asia with which Turkey had close ethnic, religious, linguistic and cultural bonds was accepted as a window of opportunity which, if successfully utilized, would provide the country a new leverage in its dealings with the Western world. This view had a positive resonance among the Western capitals as well. Turkey with its parliamentary democracy, market economy, secular stance and close alignment with the Western world could help these states in their political and economic restructuring and reintegration into the international system as independent actors. The main motive of the USA and the EU in broaching a more active and interested Turkish role in Eurasia was their apprehension about a possible creation of an Iranian sphere of influence in the region while the Russian control and power was receding.

Turkey has been resorting to political and economic instruments to increase its impact and visibility in the South Caucasus and Central Asia since the early 1990s. The organization of Turkic summits with the participation of Azerbaijan and the four Turkic republics of Kazakhstan, Uzbekistan, Turkmenistan and Kyrgyzstan, revival and expansion of the Economic Cooperation Organization (ECO) to include Azerbaijan and the Central Asian countries, and the suggestion of regional cooperation schemes such as the Caucasus Peace and Stability Pact and Caucasus Stability and Cooperation Platform to contribute to the resolution of the regional conflicts in the South Caucasus are the major Turkish efforts in the political direction. In the economic sphere, Turkey focused on positioning itself as the regional hub for energy and transport projects which would integrate the South Caucasus and Central Asia with the West. Ankara also strove to improve bilateral trade ties and encouraged Turkish businessmen to make investments in the region.

The South Caucasus and Central Asia had remained under the firm grip of the Tsarist empire, then with the Soviet Union in nineteenth century up until the early 1990s. Russia, similar to its predecessors, demonstrated a renewed interest and engagement in the affairs of its former possessions after a brief period of hesitation, confusion and internal turmoil. All the official military, national security and foreign policy documents issued in Russia in the previous two decades portrayed the South Caucasus and Central Asia as areas which were historically in Russia's sphere of interest. Russia would be responsible for bringing an end to the military clashes and conflicts erupting in its Near Abroad and preventing them from spreading onto Russian territory. Furthermore, this region sheltered 25 million Russians, was replete with rich oil and gas resources and was a significant market for Russian products and services. All these factors engendered an assertive and interventionist foreign policy on the Russian side which made use of all available political, economic and military means to reinstate its sphere of influence in the South Caucasus and Central Asia.

Russia preferred controlled instability in the South Caucasus and provided covert and overt military support to the secessionist forces in Azerbaijan and Georgia. In the economic realm, Moscow deftly captured the strategic assets of Armenia and Georgia in exchange for the unpaid debts of these countries to Russia. Russian Central Asian policy concentrated on attempts to consolidate its position through beefing up bilateral political, economic and military ties with the regional states as well as leading regional security and economic cooperation through Collective Security Treaty Organization (CSTO) and Eurasian Economic Community (EurAsEC). In Central Asia Turkey conceded that Russia had the upper hand owing to its close relations with the political elites, long-standing economic bonds with the region and its still prevalent cultural influence. However, time showed that Moscow was not a lonely player in the Central Asian game as it had to compete intensely both with the USA and China to sustain its influence in the region.

The focal point of the Turkish–Russian competition in Eurasia became South Caucasus. The two sides backed up different sides in the local conflicts and tried to infuse into the region via economic channels. This chapter will look into the details of this Turkish–Russian rivalry in the South Caucasus which has emerged as one of the major points of discord between the two countries in the post-Cold War era.

The territories of Nagorno-Karabakh, Abkhazia and South Ossetia that became disputed, as a result of the borders drawn up by the Soviet Union, appeared as the most decisive factors which determined both intra-regional relations as well as South Caucasian states' ties with the regional actors and global powers in the post-Cold War period. The following two parts will focus on Turkish and Russian policies with regard to these issue areas and to what extent they converged or diverged from each other.

Nagorno-Karabakh: The Gordian knot of the South Caucasus

The historical background of the conflict

Nagorno-Karabakh was declared an autonomous region within Azerbaijan in 1923 by the Soviet administration. Political and cultural autonomy was granted to the predominantly Armenian population. However, the Armenians never came to terms with the status of the region and occasionally accused the Azerbaijani authorities of economic discrimination, cultural denial and Azeri-biased demographic settlement. By taking advantage of the softening political atmosphere as a result of the glasnost policy of Mikhail Gorbachev, the local Soviet of Nagorno-Karabakh passed a resolution on February 20, 1988 which asked for the transfer of oblast from Azerbaijan to Armenia. On June 15, 1988 the Armenian Soviet declared its approval of Nagorno-Karabakh's call for unification with Yerevan (Herzig 1999, 13).

The Azerbaijani administration had interpreted the resolution as illegal and rejected it on June 13, 1988 (Panossian 2002, 144). According to the Article 78 of the 1977 Soviet Constitution, the boundaries between Union Republics were only altered by mutual agreement of the republics concerned, subject to ratification by the Supreme Soviet (Constitution of Soviet Socialist Republics 1977). Moscow was opposed to any territorial changes in the Soviet Union and announced on July 18, 1988 that the Nagorno-Karabakh would stay within the borders of Azerbaijan (Suny 1996, 398).

The scrimmages between Azerbaijanis and Armenians over Nagorno-Karabakh turned into a fully fledged war in 1992, right after the disintegration of the Soviet Union. The Nagorno-Karabakh paramilitary units with the help of Armenian and Russian forces won a quick and decisive triumph against the dispersed and disorganized Azerbaijani army. In addition to the Nagorno-Karabakh enclave, the seven neighboring districts[1] which were made up of Azeris were occupied and residents of these towns that were roughly 1 million had to flee to Azerbaijan. Armenian forces also managed to capture strategic points such as Lachin and Kelbejar which linked Nagorno-Karabakh directly to Armenia and Fizuli that provided Azerbaijan's access to Nakhichevan.

A ceasefire was brokered by Russia on May 12, 1994 and the political settlement of the conflict was relegated to the Organization for Security and Cooperation in Europe (OSCE) Minsk Group that was co-chaired by the USA, Russia and France.[2] The Group has not yet come up with an arrangement which can lead to the peaceful and permanent solution of the dispute. Azerbaijan's nearly 20 percent of territory is still under control of Armenians and the country shelters thousands of refugees and internally displaced people.

The Russian position vis-à-vis the stalemate and its implications on relations with Azerbaijan and Armenia

Cognizant of the fact that a resource-rich Azerbaijan might distance itself from the orbit of Russia in the near future, especially when the pro-Turkish and pro-Western Abulfaz Elchibey was in power, Moscow supported the separatist movement in Nagorno-Karabakh by sending weapons, military equipment and mercenaries from the 366th Motorized Rifle Regiment in Stepanakert, the 7th Army in Yerevan and the 4th Army in Ganja (Goltz 1993, 98) in order to weaken the government in Baku and make it more malleable to Russian onslaughts. The loss of Nagorno-Karabakh to the Armenians brought the end of the presidency of Elchibey and he was replaced by Heydar Aliyev in October 1993. Both Heydar Aliyev during his ten-year tenure and his son Ilham Aliyev who succeeded him in 2003 have been attaching great importance to pursuing balanced and cautious policies toward Russia. In this context, although Azerbaijan participated to the Russian-led Commonwealth of Independent States (CIS) in December 1993, a few months after Heydar Aliyev was inaugurated as President of Azerbaijan, it eschewed partaking in its military arm, the CSTO. Moreover, Heydar Aliyev also dragged his feet on allowing Russia to build up military bases on Azerbaijani territory and send Russian peacekeeping forces to Nagorno-Karabakh. However, mostly stemming from the reason not to enrage Russia, Azerbaijan did not seriously seek NATO membership opposed to Georgia, although it had signed a Partnership for Peace (PfP) agreement with the Alliance in 1994.

Azerbaijan steers the middle course in its economic relations with Russia as well. Energy cooperation constitutes epicenter of the economic association between Baku and Moscow. Azerbaijan, while taking part in Western-backed oil and natural gas projects such as Baku-Tbilisi-Ceyhan (BTC) and Baku-Tbilisi-Erzurum (BTE), has been operating the Baku-Novorossiysk oil pipeline with Russia for a long time and has also been providing gas supplies to Moscow since 2010. Furthermore, Azerbaijan is the most important trade partner of Russia in the South Caucasus; the bilateral trade between the two countries reached 2.6 billion dollars in 2013 ("Russia-Azerbaijan Trade" 2014).

Russia's incessant scuffling with Georgia and the country's stubborn policies toward integration with the Western structures coupled with Azerbaijan's offish demeanor emanating from its increasing wealth thanks to oil and gas revenues led the Russian foreign policy-makers turn to Armenia and put this country at the center of their strategy with regard to South Caucasus. Armenia, with its position as a barrier between Turkey and Azerbaijan and its serious problems with these states, became a useful ally for Russian moves in the region in the post-Cold War period. In September 1992, the two countries signed a pact which delegated patrolling of Turkish and Iranian frontiers to Russian border guards (Masih and Krikorian 1999, 105). The agreement of March 1995 enabled Russia to keep military bases in Yerevan and Gyumri for 25 years (Robins 2003, 169). With an agreement signed on August 20, 2010, in the course of Russian President Medvedev's visit to Armenia, Russia's leasing rights in military bases in Armenia were extended to 2044 (President of Russia 2010). Armenia is also a member of the Russian-led military organizations such as CSTO, and the Armenian army is heavily equipped with Russian arms and military equipment (Danielyan 2016). Furthermore, the two countries signed an agreement in December 2015 to create a joint air-defense system ("Armenia Ratifies" 2016).

The Russian–Armenian bilateral trade reached to 1.2 billion dollars in 2012 (Anishchuk 2013). Russia captured significant assets in energy, banking and financial services, telecommunications, mining, manufacturing and transportation sectors of the Armenian economy in return for Yerevan's swelling debt resulting from unpaid natural gas, fuel oil and electricity bills. More than 1 million Armenians live in Russia and the remittances they send to their home country made up 5 percent of Armenia's gross domestic product in 2012 ("Private Remittances" 2013). Armenia also participated to the Russian-led Eurasian Economic Union (EEU) in December 2014 (Herszenhorn 2014) which also included Belarus and Kazakhstan.

While Armenia is largely under its control both in military and economic terms and Azerbaijan seriously takes into account Russian sensitivities when formulating energy and defense policies, it is not surprising that Russia is content with the status quo in Nagorno-Karabakh and is not eager to push for resolution of the conflict which will reduce both Armenia's dependence on its guardianship and will trigger more independent foreign policy line in Azerbaijan. So Russia's gathering up of Armenian and Azerbaijan presidents under its auspices in trilateral meetings since November 2008 can be taken as more of a temporizing act rather than genuine maneuver toward the peaceful settlement of the Nagorno-Karabakh issue as despite the convocation of these meetings no concrete step has been taken up to now for the resolution of the impasse.

The Turkish standing regarding the conundrum and its rapprochement efforts with Armenia

The Turkish position concerning the Nagorno-Karabakh problem has been so far clearly in favor of Azerbaijan. Turkey supported the Azerbaijani claims regarding the district and closed its border with Armenia in 1993 in solidarity with Baku. Azerbaijan is more valuable for Turkey compared to Armenia because of the former's close ethnic, religious and cultural ties it entertained with Turkey as well as Baku being in possession of rich energy resources that could be transmitted to international markets through Turkey which would not only provide the country transportation revenue but also would boost Ankara's geostrategic importance. However, Turkey also backed mediation attempts to solve the Nagorno-Karabakh conflict whole-heartedly as the resolution of this grueling problem in a way that was acceptable to both Armenia and Azerbaijan would precipitate a thaw between the two countries and pave the way for economic and social integration of Turkey and the regional states and would also help Turkey and Armenia to overcome their bilateral troublesome history. Turkey also took some steps to relax the embargo it imposed on Armenia and worked to restore Armenian religious monuments in Anatolia. Armenia opened its first official representative office in Turkey in 2002 within BSEC ("Armenia Opens" 2002). Turkey initiated cargo transportation from Yerevan to İstanbul as well as charter flights between Yerevan and Antalya (Bozkuş 2008). Akdamar Church in Van, Armenian Catholic Church in Diyarbakır and the Armenian Church in Ordu were renovated by the Turkish government (Aras and Akpınar 2011, 61). However, Turkey's efforts toward reconciliation with Armenia sufficed neither for alleviation of the bilateral issues between the two states nor brought out any breakthrough for settlement of the Nagorno-Karabakh conflict. Turkey's last attempt to mend fences with Armenia through the signing of two protocols on October 10, 2009 in Switzerland within the presence of high-profile figures from the international community was also aborted after it was clearly understood that Armenia did not have any intention of putting an end to its occupation of Azerbaijani territories. Armenia continues to stick to its state policy of international recognition of the so-called genocide that is enforced hand in hand with diaspora groups which puts further strain on its relations with Turkey.

Despite the souring of the Turkish-Azerbaijani relationship as a result of Turkey's short-lived opening to Armenia, Turkey and Azerbaijan got over the crisis quickly and continued their cooperation in energy and transportation projects. The BTC pipeline, which eradicated Russia's monopoly position in energy transportation in the Caspian Basin, was inaugurated in May 2005. The second component of the East–West energy corridor, BTE Natural Gas Pipeline became operational in July 2007. Consistent with an intergovernmental agreement clinched between Greece and Turkey on February 23, 2003, the Azeri gas commenced to flow into Europe through the Turkey–Greece–Italy Interconnector Pipeline from November 18, 2007 ("Türkiye-Yunanistan Doğalgaz" 2007). The two countries signed another intergovernmental agreement in the field of energy in October 2011 which set the conditions for the sale of Azerbaijani gas to Turkey from the Shah Deniz-2 project starting from 2017 as well the transit of the same gas to Turkey via the networks of BOTAŞ in 2017–2042 (SOCAR 2011). Moreover, on December 26, 2011, a memorandum of understanding to build Trans–Anatolian Natural Gas Pipeline to transfer Azerbaijani natural gas to Europe through Turkish territory was signed by Turkish minister of energy Taner Yıldız and his Azerbaijani equivalent Natig Aliyev which would further strengthen the energy ties between the two countries. Turkey and Azerbaijan also collaborate in a regional transportation scheme, the Baku–Tbilisi–Kars (BTK) railroad project which is planned to be finished in 2017. Bilateral trade between Turkey and Azerbaijan hit nearly three billion dollars in 2014 (Turkish Institute of Statistics 2015) making Azerbaijan Turkey's most important trade partner in the South Caucasus.

In the military sphere, Turkey continued to provide financial aid, logistical and technical assistance and technical training to the Azerbaijani armed forces. The two states also began to engage in a partnership pertaining to arms production. Turkish weapons manufacturer and defense contractor Roketsan and Azerbaijani military scientific and industrial enterprise Iglim reached an agreement on joint production of rocket launcher systems in March 2009. In accordance with the deal, rocket launchers, some parts and molds of some arms would be made at the Iglim enterprise and rockets would be manufactured at the plants of Roketsan in Turkey. The first large-size delivery of missiles from Roketsan to Azerbaijan took place in February 2012 (Ergan 2012). In a similar way, the Ministry of Defense Industry of Azerbaijan and Turkey's Otokar signed a protocol of intention in October 2010 to produce armored equipment (Suleymanov 2010).

The Turkish–Russian competition over Nagorno-Karabakh

The Nagorno-Karabakh issue has become a matter of contention between Turkey and Russia since its outbreak at the beginning of the 1990s. The two countries also exchanged a few hard words during the hot stage of the conflict. When Turkish President Turgut Özal stated in May 1992 that Ankara ought to send troops to protect Nakhichevan, the Azerbaijani enclave inside Armenia that also bordered Turkey and whose territorial integrity was guaranteed by Ankara according to the Kars Agreement signed between Turkey and Soviet Union in 1921, in the case of a possible Armenian occupation of the land, Yevgeny Shaposhnikov, the last defense minister of the Soviet Union and Commander-in-Chief of the armed forces of the CIS declared that if there was military interference by another party, that would precipitate a third world war which would drag in all the global powers into the conflict (Goldberg 1992). Later, in April 1993, Özal accused Russia of supporting the Karabakh Armenians following the capture of Kelbejar by the Armenian forces and hinted at closer military relations with Azerbaijan including arm support. In response, Russian Defense Minister Grachev warned Ankara to stay out of Azerbaijan during his visit to Turkey (Pry 1999, 123).

The Demirel government in Turkey, however, chose not to push the battle of words with Russia too far. It was clear that Russia was superior to Turkey in terms of diplomatic influence and military capacity. Besides, economic and military bonds were flourishing between the two countries at a steady pace in the early 1990s. Many Turkish companies, especially the construction firms, had set foot on the nascent yet promising Russian market and commenced business in the country. The Turkish–Russian trade exceeded two billion dollars in 1993 and Russia became the sixth biggest trade partner of Turkey. Moreover, in the same year Turkey started to purchase weapons and military hardware from Russia, when her European and American allies had refused to provide military equipment to Ankara that would be used in its struggle with PKK.

The Nagorno-Karabakh dispute entered a cooling period with the signing of the ceasefire agreement in 1994 and Russia and Turkey did not squabble over the conflict in public again. However, the two countries had different opinions regarding the resolution of the problem and this divergence of opinion came to the surface from time to time. Turkey gave its full countenance to Armenian-Azeri parley to resolve the Nagorno-Karabakh deadlock as the settlement of this issue in a way acceptable to both Azerbaijan and Armenia would also open the path for normalization of complicated and thorny relations between Turkey and Armenia and would expedite Armenia's participation to energy and transportation projects spearheaded by Turkey in the South Caucasus. Moreover, in the case of the resolution of the conflict, Turkey would be able to re-open its border with Armenia without facing much objection from the Azerbaijani side which would eliminate the criticisms directed against her from the EU and USA with regard to the closed border gates between the neighbors.

In line with this reasoning, Ankara has supported meetings that were conducted through informal channels to find reconciliation between Armenia and Azerbaijan pertaining to the Nagorno-Karabakh conflict starting from the late 1990s. It gave its approval to the proposed land-swap deal that came to the negotiating table in 1999 which included unification of Armenia with Nagorno-Karabakh in return for ceding the Meghri district in Armenia to Azerbaijan which would secure Azerbaijan's direct access to Nakhichevan (Libaridian 2007, 262). After this plan was rejected by the parties, Ankara initiated a trilateral dialogue between Turkey, Armenia and Azerbaijan and the foreign ministers of three countries İsmail Cem, Vardan Oskanian and Vilayet Guliyev met on May 15, 2002, during the meeting of NATO Foreign Ministers in Reykjavik ("Turkish, Armenian, Azeri" 2002). However, these Turkish efforts proved to be impotent in creating a significant breakthrough in bringing out a desired solution to the Nagorno-Karabakh issue.

The impetus to reach reconciliation in Turkish-Armenian relations gained steam with induction of Serzh Sargsyan as the new head of state of Armenia in April 2008 following the February 2008 presidential election. The Turkish President Abdullah Gül became one of the first leaders who congratulated Sargsyan on his election victory. On July 9, 2008, in an article published on the *Wall Street Journal*, Sargsyan extended an invitation to Gül to watch the World Cup qualifier football match that would take place in Yerevan between the Armenian and Turkish national football teams on September 6, 2008 (Sargsyan 2008). Gül accepted the invitation and became the first Turkish President that ever visited Armenia.

Most of Armenia's fuel and much of its grain came through Georgia's Black Sea ports, and containment of the country deepened during the Georgian–Russian fight of August 2008 as a key railway bridge between Armenia and Georgia was mined and the port of Poti remained occupied by Russian troops. The disruption in Armenia's trade levels and the flight of international investors made Yerevan more amenable and willing to look for an accommodation with Ankara. The negotiations conducted under the auspices of Swiss mediation culminated in the signing of two protocols on October 10, 2009, which anticipated the establishment and development of diplomatic relations between Turkey and Armenia along with the opening of the common border between the two countries within two months. There was not any mention of the Nagorno-Karabakh issue in the protocols. However, Turkish officials claimed that they explicitly conveyed the message to their Armenian counterparts that the activation of the protocols would be dependent on progress on the resolution of the Nagorno-Karabakh conflict (Phillips 2012, 47–8). Neither Azerbaijan nor the opposition parties in Turkey were satisfied with these explanations. Baku immediately and strongly denounced the protocols considering them as a major blow to its policy regarding Nagorno-Karabakh. Furthermore, Azerbaijan resorted to punitive measures against Turkey on the economic platform and raised the price of natural gas sold to Ankara. The leaders of the major opposition parties in Turkey, Deniz Baykal and Devlet Bahçeli, on the other hand, accused the government of selling out the national cause and leaving Azerbaijan in the cold. In the following months after Armenia made it clear that it would not accept any preconditions for the development of its diplomatic relations with Turkey, regarding it as linking of the reconciliation process with Turkey to progress on the settlement of the Nagorno-Karabakh matter, the Turkish government could not risk further estrangement of Azerbaijan amidst intense domestic objection and eschewed bringing in the protocols to the Turkish Grand National Assembly for ratification. After dragging for a few months, the Turkish–Armenian rapprochement process halted in April 2010, subsequent to Yerevan's declaration of suspension of the ratification procedure in the Armenian Parliament. This last failed attempt demonstrated once and for all that the foundation of a workable relationship between Turkey and Armenia is very much contingent on reaching a permanent agreement on Nagorno-Karabakh which would be embraced by Azerbaijan wholeheartedly.

Russia, contrary to Turkey, was not in a hurry for the resolution of the Nagorno-Karabakh impasse as the current situation ensured considerable Russian control and influence both on Baku and Yerevan. Armenia granted Russia complete military and economic dominance on its territory in exchange of protection against Azerbaijan and Turkey, both of which sealed off its borders with Yerevan following the outbreak of the Nagorno-Karabakh conflict. Armenia also demonstrates its gratitude to Moscow by being a loyal member of the Russian-led security and economic organizations such as the CSTO and the EEU.

Azerbaijan, on the other hand, is extremely careful not to antagonize Russia, although its relationship with Moscow cannot be described as intense and intimate as Armenia's. Despite the fact that Azerbaijan has been involved in NATO's PfP program for more than 20 years and has also participated in the Alliance's Afghanistan and Kosovo operations, top officials in the country often feel the need to underline that Baku does not have any aspirations to join NATO (Kucera 2013). Furthermore, Azerbaijan's decision to decline signing the Association Agreement with the EU in the framework of the Eastern Partnership and instead settling for a visa simplification arrangement in September 2014 earned appreciation and approval from Moscow (Ibrahimov 2014).

Being well aware of Russia's deep impact especially on Armenia, Turkey called on Moscow to play a more active role in resolving the Nagorno-Karabakh conflict following the failure of the protocols. However, neither Putin nor foreign minister Sergey Lavrov accepted any linkage between the Nagorno-Karabakh issue and the Turkish-Armenian rapprochement and refused to exert any pressure on Armenia (Weitz 2010, 76–7). Nevertheless, following the Turkish attempt to reach a compromise with Armenia, Russia made a counter riposte and gathered together Aliyev and Sargsyan in Kremlin in the company of President Medvedev on November 2, 2008. At the end of the convocation, the parties released a declaration which accentuated that they would pursue a political settlement for the resolution of the matter (President of Russia 2008a). However, the succeeding trilateral meetings were far from bringing any tangible development toward the resolution of the conflict.

Russia gave its approval and blessing to the Turkish–Armenian rapprochement because it figured out that the agreed protocols did not foresee any articles that related the compromise process to the resolution of the Nagorno-Karabakh problem. Moreover, the protocols' implementation would not reduce Russia's influence in Armenia, quite the opposite. In the case of establishment of economic relations between Turkey and Armenia, Russia would be the chief beneficiary of the process because Moscow had secured a strong economic presence in the country through appropriation of major energy and transport assets of Yerevan. So it was hardly surprising that Russian Foreign Minister Lavrov participated to the signing ceremony of the protocols that was held in Switzerland in October 2009 and urged Armenian minister of foreign affairs Edward Nalbandian to sign the deal in a strongly worded note ("Krizi Lavrov" 2009).

Russia also anticipated that decoupling the Nagorno-Karabakh issue from the Turkish-Armenian reconciliation in the protocols would sow discord between Turkey and Azerbaijan and would create an environment that would work to the benefit of Moscow. This proved to be true as four days after the signing of the protocols, Azerbaijan agreed to sell at least 500 million cubic meters of natural gas to Russia per annum starting from 2010 (Bodansky 2010). Aliyev also declared his country's support for South Stream gas pipeline project promoted by Russia and added that Baku postponed the development of Shah Deniz gas field until 2017 (Phillips 2012, 62) which was expected to be the major source of natural gas for the EU and Turkey backed Nabucco gas pipeline scheme.

It has become clear that Turkey and Russia have different and mutually exclusive views, positions and interests with regard to the Nagorno-Karabakh matter. They are far from forming common institutions or joint mechanisms which could contribute through provision of regular communication, consultation and bargaining opportunities as well as introduction of political initiatives to the enduring and peaceful settlement of the conflict. The dispute seems to remain as one of the most significant points of disagreement between the two countries in the post-Cold War era.

Abkhazia and South Ossetia: Divergent Standings

Georgia plays a critical role in the South Caucasus region with its strategic location as a transit country. Important oil and gas pipelines and railway systems traverse its territory; the country has direct access to the Black Sea and the other South Caucasian states. Azerbaijan and Armenia rely on Georgia for transportation. Tbilisi also retains a significant place in the South Caucasian policies of Moscow and Ankara. Starting from the beginning of the 1990s, the two countries have adopted different views regarding the future of this small state. While Turkey stressed the territorial integrity of Georgia and the inviolability of its borders owing to its important energy and transportation projects with this country, Russia encouraged the separatist aspirations of breakaway regions of Abkhazia and South Ossetia in order to prevent Georgia drifting away from its orbit and drawing near to Western political and security structures.

Russia's approach to Abkhazia and South Ossetia

Military conflicts flared up both in Abkhazia and South Ossetia just after the breakup of the Soviet Union. Russia, as with to the Nagorno-Karabakh case, lent a hand to the separatist forces through military and material means, mediated the ceasefire negotiations between the warring parties and ensured the deployment of CIS peacekeeping forces which were overwhelmingly composed of Russian soldiers to both of the regions. Georgia abandoned its reluctance regarding participation to CIS at the end of the war in Abkhazia and South Ossetia and conceded to establishment of Russian economic dominance in these areas in exchange for Moscow's withdrawal of further support to the independence aspirations of these secessionist entities.

In the following years Georgia set to make moves to dissociate itself from the grip of Russia and searched for closer cooperation with the Western world, especially with the USA and the NATO. American military instructors came to the country in February 2002 in order to train nearly 2,000 Georgian special forces within the framework of Train and Equip program (Naumkin 2002, 34) and with a bilateral security pact that was ratified by the Georgian Parliament in late March 2003 the American military personnel were permitted visa-free entry and exit from the country, to carry weapons and to deploy military hardware (Chigorin 2003, 130). Georgia succeeded in closing down the Russian military bases of Akhalkalaki, Batumi and Vaziani. Tbilisi also condoned the settling of Chechen militants in the Pankisi Gorge where Georgian citizens of Chechen origin called Kists resided (Baran 2002, 224) in retaliation for Russian aid to the separatist currents in Abkhazia and South Ossetia.

Russian–Georgian relations turned into a more grueling and problematical form after Mikheil Saakashvili became the Head of State of Georgia in January 2004. Saakashvili's efforts to forge closer ties with the USA and the EU and Georgia's relentless drive to join NATO incited an explicit demur on the Russian side whereas Moscow's continuing shoring up of secessionist districts of Abkhazia and South Ossetia morally and materially further enraged Georgia and made it increase its efforts to distance itself from Russia.

The Russian-Georgian relations reached to their lowest ebb in the summer of 2008 when Georgia commenced a military offensive on August 7 to reassert its authority in South Ossetia. The operation sparked an adamant and livid retort from Russia, and Moscow went to support the separatist province with troops, naval force, military aircraft and tanks (Antonenko 2008, 26). After a five-day war in which

Russia not only expelled the Georgian forces from Abkhazia and South Ossetia but also invaded Georgia proper, Georgian government declared a unilateral ceasefire. With the stepping in of French President Nicolas Sarkozy, Georgia and Russia agreed on an armistice on August 12, 2008 and Russia began to pull its military units out from Georgian territory (Nagle 2008, 74).

On August 14, 2008, the Parliament of Georgia adopted resolutions terminating the country's membership to CIS (Ministry of Foreign Affairs of Georgia 2008). This was followed by Russia's recognition of the independence of Abkhazia and South Ossetia on August 26, 2008 and establishment of diplomatic relations with these two entities on September 9, 2008 (President of Russia 2008b). Although Russia imputed its decision to hostile and irresponsible acts of the Georgian leadership to the peoples of Abkhazia and South Ossetia, it had already entered into a process of de-facto recognition of Abkhazia and South Ossetia in reaction to Georgia's push to receive a NATO Membership Action Plan and international acknowledgement of the unilateral declaration of independence of Kosovo. On April 16, 2008, the Russian president signed a decree which envisaged direct official relations between Russian government bodies in the North Caucasus and the secessionist authorities in Abkhazia and South Ossetia. The edict recognized the legal acts issued by Abkhazian and South Ossetian officials and entities registered under Abkhaz and South Ossetian laws. The statute also called on Russian authorities to provide legal assistance on matters of civil and criminal law directly to Abkhazian and South Ossetian executives and residents (Corso 2008). It can be said that Georgia's August 2008 military incursion to South Ossetia did not induce, but quickened Russia's decision of recognition.

Moscow's fierce and fiery reaction to Georgia's attempt to regain the control of its breakaway province of South Ossetia demonstrated once and for all that Russia was ready to show muscle if it believed that vital interests were at stake in the South Caucasus region. With its military incursion to Georgia, Russia not only managed to halt Georgia's NATO membership but also consolidated its military outreach in Abkhazia and South Ossetia. Russia established the 7th Military Base in Gudauta in Abkhazia and 4th Military Base in Djava and Tskhinvali in South Ossetia in the wake of the 2008 war. Both of the bases are part of the Russian North Caucasus Military District and host nearly 4,000 Russian soldiers (German 2012, 1653–4). Russia also commenced the construction of a naval base in Ochamchire, Abkhazia in June 2012. Finally, with the agreements signed with Abkhazia in 2014 (President of Russia 2014) and with South Ossetia in 2015 (President of

Russia 2015), Russia was granted the privilege to co-determine foreign policy as well as to develop defense and security space in these secessionist regions which included joint-protection of borders with Georgia.

Despite the periodic disruption in gas supply, frequent electricity cut-offs and price hikes, Russia held the ground in Georgia by preserving its position as the country's chief energy provider. Moscow also captured the energy infrastructure of Tbilisi by acquiring the controlling stakes in gas and power companies in Georgia. Russian companies also laid hands on the financial sector of Georgia. In January 2005, Russia's state-controlled Vneshtorgbank bought 51 percent of the shares of the United Georgian Bank, one of the three leading banks in Georgia (Anjaparidze 2005). Russia managed to become the fourth biggest trade partner of Georgia in 2013 with 780 million dollar worth trade although the figures remained much lower than its trade with Armenia and Azerbaijan ("Georgia's Foreign Trade" 2014).

Turkey's approach to Abkhazia and South Ossetia

Turkey, contrary to Russia, has been sticking to its policy of defending the sovereignty and territorial integrity of Georgia since the early 1990s despite the calls in the opposite direction coming from its North Caucasian community. Georgia is a key state for Turkey's BTC and BTE energy pipeline and BTK railway projects. The trade volume between Turkey and Georgia came at one and a half billion dollars in 2013 ("Georgia's Foreign Trade" 2014); Turkey sustained its first place as the largest trade partner of Georgia. The lifting of visa requirements for Georgian and Turkish citizens in February 2006, signing the Free Trade Agreement and Agreement on Avoidance of Double Taxation in November 2007 and finally inking an agreement in May 2011 between the two states which allowed citizens of both countries' to visit each other's state by showing just a national identity card facilitated further strengthening of commercial and people-to-people ties between Turkey and Georgia (Republic of Turkey Ministry of Foreign Affairs 2013).

Ankara also developed bilateral military relations with Tbilisi. Turkey extended financial help, material and technical property, and training programs to the Georgian army. Training centers were constructed in Kodori and Gori along with a shooting range outside Tbilisi (Larrabee and Lesser 2002, 105–6). Turkey also helped the Georgian government with reconstruction of the Vaziani military base and repair and modernization of the military airbase in Marneuli.

Georgia, along with Azerbaijan, served as part of the Turkish contingent in the NATO-led peacekeeping operation in Kosovo.

The 2008 war put Turkey in a very difficult position due to the fact that despite its economic and military investments in Georgia, Ankara was in no way to confront Russia directly because of its elevated political and economic ties with Moscow. Therefore, Turkey during the war went to great lengths to strike a fine balance in its dealings with Russia and Georgia. Ankara was among the first to send humanitarian aid to Georgia in the form of food, drinking water, disposable medical goods, tents and blankets in the wake of the military clashes and also declared on August 26, 2008, that it attached importance to the independence, sovereignty and territorial integrity of Georgia (Republic of Turkey Ministry of Foreign Affairs 2008). On the other hand, Turkey took into consideration Russian concerns regarding the USA entry into Black Sea with two large warships to bring in humanitarian assistance to Tbilisi and persuaded Washington to send in smaller ships whose total weight did not exceed the maximum limit defined by the Montreux Convention.

Another important Turkish initiative during the Russian–Georgian conflict of August 2008 was Ankara's suggestion to establish the Caucasus Stability and Cooperation Platform which would include Armenia, Azerbaijan, and Georgia along with Russia and Turkey that would act as a forum for dialogue for regional countries and would make them to sit around a table and discuss their mutual severe problems. Turkey had proposed a similar Caucasus Peace and Stability Pact back in January 2000 but the difference of the 2008 pact from its predecessor became the exclusion of the USA, the EU and the OSCE from the proposed regional scheme.

This new situation was appealing for Moscow as it always frowned on any kind of American or European interest and involvement in the South Caucasus. When Turkish President Demirel had launched Caucasus Peace and Stability Pact in January 2000 during his visit to Georgia, Moscow officially welcomed Demirel's proposal but frankly expressed its discomfort at the prospect of American involvement in the scheme. The Chief of the Main Department of International Cooperation at the Russian Defense Ministry, Colonel General Leonid Ivashov, had even announced that the USA and NATO should not be allowed to participate in the creation of a security system in the Caucasus as the involvement of Americans in the South Caucasus would not improve the security of the region (Tamrazian 2000). Eight years later, Turkish Premier Erdoğan unveiled the Caucasus Stability and Cooperation Platform in Moscow after his meeting with Russian

President Medvedev and Prime Minister Putin and then revealed it to Saakashvili and Aliyev. The American side was quite stunned as understood from Deputy State Secretary Matthew Bryza's statement that they thought Turkey and the USA had agreed upon their policy in the South Caucasian region. However, Ankara had not informed Washington about the matter, and they were very surprised with their partner's actions (Aliyev 2008). Turkey was in pursuit of restoration of peace and stability in the South Caucasus which would serve best to its political and economic interests in the region and became convinced after the August 2008 war that any regional scheme that excluded Russia would have slim chance of success. Therefore, it was not that unexpected for Ankara to seek Russian endorsement before disclosing its proposed regional structure.

However, being in the same organization with an aggressive and resurgent Russia was not encouraging for two of the invitees of the pact, that is to say, Azerbaijan and Georgia. Furthermore, Azerbaijan and Armenia were hardly on speaking terms due to the deadlock in the Nagorno-Karabakh issue and Turkey's short-lived rapprochement attempt with Armenia backfired as well. Thus, the second Turkish initiative shared the fate of the first and could not bring together the contested parties in a regional framework which would be conducive to the establishment of order and stability in the South Caucasus region.

Post-Cold War developments showed that the South Caucasus region is a point of serious discord and competition between Turkey and Russia. Turkey boosted its political and economic ties with Azerbaijan and Georgia and made some headway in military cooperation with these states. Russia sustained its economic and military dominance in Armenia when Yerevan failed to reach a compromise with its two neighbors Azerbaijan and Turkey on the Nagorno-Karabakh dispute. Despite the breakdown of the political relations with Georgia as a result of the August 2008 war, Russia managed to penetrate the region economically through its natural gas exports to Armenia and Georgia and via appropriation of Armenian and Georgian companies in various sectors in return of unpaid debts of these states to Russia.

The post-Cold War era witnessed divergence of Turkish and Russian views, positions and approaches with regard to the Nagorno-Karabakh, Abkhazia and South Ossetia issues. The inability of Ankara and Moscow to form a regional cooperation mechanism that could act as a barrier against the outbreak of these conflicts in the South Caucasus demonstrated that developing political relations and strong economic ties between Turkey and Russia has not yet sufficed to overcome the existing rivalry and divergent foreign policy lines in the region.

The next chapter will focus on another region of prominence for both Turkey and Russia in the post-Cold War period: Central Asia. Here, however, the competition was less intense and vocal and the two parties managed to overcome their differences to some extent and come together under the roof a regional cooperation organization.

Notes

1 These are Agdam, Fizuli, Jabrail, Kelbejar, Kubatly, Lachin and Zangelan.
2 The other participating states of the Minsk Group are Belarus, Finland, Germany, Italy, the Netherlands, Portugal, Sweden and Turkey.

References

Aliyev, Mehman. 2008. "From Balkan Pact to Stability for Caucasus." *Azeri Report*, September 29.
Anishchuk, Alexei. 2013. "Russia's Putin Faces Protests as He Woos Armenia." *Reuters*, December 2.
Anjaparidze, Zaal. 2005. "Russia Claims Strategic Victory in Georgian Privatization Round." *Eurasia Daily Monitor* 2(22), January 31.
Antonenko, Oksana. 2008. "A War with No Winners." *Survival* 5(5): 23–36.
Aras, Bülent, and Pınar Akpınar. 2011. "The Relations between Turkey and the Caucasus." *Perceptions (Journal of International Affairs)* 16(3): 53–68.
Asbarez, "Armenia Opens First Ever Mission in Turkey." 2002. March 4.
Baran, Zeyno. 2002. "The Caucasus: Ten Years after Independence." *The Washington Quarterly* 25(1): 221–234.
Bodansky, Yossef. 2010. "Europe's Latest Tinder Box and Global Mega Trends – Russia's Pre-eminence in the EU Energy Market." *OilPrice.com*, April 10.
Bozkuş, Yıldız Deveci. 2008. "Türkiye'den Bir Adım Daha: Erivan-Antalya Uçak Seferleri." *ASAM*, July 30.
Caspian News Agency, "Turkish, Armenian, Azeri Foreign Ministers Hold First Tripartite Meeting." 2002. May 16.
Chigorin, Aleksandr. 2003. "Russian-Georgian Relations." *International Affairs (Moscow)* 49(4): 125–138.
Civil Georgia, "Georgia's Foreign Trade in 2013." 2014. January 24.
CNNTurk, "Krizi Lavrov mu Çözdü: "Sakince İmzala ve Git ..."2009. October 12.
Constitution of Soviet Socialist Republics. 1977. Bucknell University. Accessed March 24, 2013. http://www.departments.bucknell.edu/russian/const/77cons03.html/.
Corso, Molly. 2008. "Georgia Holds Steady As Moscow Inches Closer to Abkhazia, South Ossetia." *Eurasia Insight*, April 17.
Danielyan, Emil. 2016. "Russia Details Fresh Arms Supplies to Armenia." *Azatutyun*, February 19.

Ergan, Uğur. 2012. "Azerbaycan Ordusuna Türk Roketi Gidiyor." *Hürriyet*, February 19.
German, Tracey. 2012. "Securing the South Caucasus: Military Aspects of Russian Policy towards the Region since 2008." *Europe-Asia Studies* 64(9): 1650–1666.
Goldberg, Carey. 1992. "Moscow Sees War Threat if Outsiders Act in Karabakh." *Los Angeles Times*, May 21.
Goltz, Thomas. 1993. "Letter from Eurasia: The Hidden Russian Hand." *Foreign Policy*, no. 92: 92–116.
Herszenhorn, David M. 2014. "Armenia Wins Backing to Join Trade Bloc Championed by Putin." *New York Times*, December 10.
Herzig, Edmund. 1999. *The New Caucasus: Armenia, Azerbaijan and Georgia*. New York: Pinter.
Hürriyet, "Türkiye-Yunanistan Doğalgaz Boru Hattı Açıldı." 2007. November 18.
Ibrahimov, Rovshan. 2014. "Russia's Borders: Azerbaijan Benefits from not Offending its More Powerful Neighbour." *The Conversation*, December 10.
Keohane, Robert O., and Joseph S. Nye Jr. 1977. *Power and Interdependence: World Politics in Transition*. Boston: Little Brown.
Kucera, Joshua. 2013. "Azerbaijan: We Want neither NATO nor CSTO – For Now." *Eurasianet*, May 26.
Larrabee, F. Stephen, and Ian O. Lesser. 2002. *Turkish Foreign Policy in an Age of Uncertainty*. Santa Monica: RAND.
Libaridian, Gerard J. 2007. *Modern Armenia: People, Nation, State*. New Brunswick: Transaction Publishers.
Masih, Joseph R., and Robert O. Krikorian. 1999. *Armenia: At the Crossroads*. Amsterdam: Harwood Academic Publishers.
Ministry of Foreign Affairs of Georgia. 2008. "Statement of the Ministry of Foreign Affairs of Georgia on Georgia's Withdrawal from CIS." *Ministry of Foreign Affairs of Georgia*. Accessed January 3, 2009. http://www.mfa.gov.ge/index.php?lang_id=ENG&sec_id=36&info_id=7526/.
Nagle, Chad. 2008. "Whither Transcaucasia." *Turkish Policy Quarterly* 7(2): 71–81.
Naumkin, Vitaly. 2002. "Russian Policy in the South Caucasus." *The Quarterly Journal*, no. 3: 31–37.
PanArmenian.Net, "Private Remittances to Armenia Total $83 Million in 2012." 2013. March 11.
Panossian, Razmik. 2002. "The Irony of Nagorno-Karabakh: Formal Institutions versus Informal Politics." In *Ethnicity and Territory in the Former Soviet Union: Regions in Conflict*, edited by James Hughes and Gwendolyn Sasse, 143–164. Portland: Frank Cass.
Phillips, David L. 2012. *Diplomatic History: The 2009 Protocol on the Establishment of Diplomatic Relations between the Republic of Armenia and the Republic of Turkey and the 2009 Protocol on the Development of Bilateral*

Relations between the Republic of Turkey and the Republic of Armenia. New York: Institute for the Study of Human Rights.
President of Russia. 2008a. "Declaration between the Republic of Azerbaijan, the Republic of Armenia and the Russian Federation." *President of Russia*. Accessed April 7, 2013. http://www.kremlin.ru/eng/text/docs/2008/11/208708.shtml/.
President of Russia. 2008b. "Statement by President of Russia Dmitry Medvedev." *President of Russia*. Accessed April 7, 2013. http://www.kremlin.ru/eng/speeches/2008/08/26/1543_type82912_205752.shtml/.
President of Russia. 2010. "Russian-Armenian Talks." *President of Russia*. Accessed April 1, 2013. http://eng.kremlin.ru/news/808/.
President of Russia. 2014. "Meeting with President of Abkhazia Raul Khadzhimba." *President of Russia*. Accessed May 17, 2015. http://en.kremlin.ru/events/president/news/47057/.
President of Russia. 2015. "Press Statement following Talks with President of South Ossetia Leonid Tibilov." *President of Russia*. Accessed May 17, 2015. http://en.kremlin.ru/events/president/transcripts/47876/.
Pry, Peter Vincent. 1999. *War Scare: Russia and America on the Nuclear Brink*. Westport: Praeger Publishers.
Republic of Turkey Ministry of Foreign Affairs. 1989. "Commission Opinion on Turkey's Request for Accession to the Community." *Republic of Turkey Ministry of Foreign Affairs*. Accessed March 16, 2013. http://www.mfa.gov.tr/commission-opinion-on-turkey_s-request-for-accession-to-the-community_-december-20_-1989.en.mfa/.
Republic of Turkey Ministry of Foreign Affairs. 2008. "Press Release Regarding the Independence of Georgia." *Republic of Turkey Ministry of Foreign Affairs*. Accessed March 14, 2009. http://www.mfa.gov.tr/no_158_-26-agustos-2008_-gurcistan_in-bagimsizligi-hk_.en.mfa/.
Republic of Turkey Ministry of Foreign Affairs. 2013. "Türkiye-Gürcistan Siyasi İlişkileri." *Republic of Turkey Ministry of Foreign Affairs*. Accessed April 7, 2013. http://www.mfa.gov.tr/turkiye-gurcistan-siyasi-iliskileri.tr.mfa/.
Reuters, "Armenia Ratifies Agreement on Joint Air-Defence System with Russia." 2016. June 30.
Robins, Philip. 2003. *Suits and Uniforms: Turkish Foreign Policy since the Cold War*. London: Hurst & Company.
Sargsyan, Serzh. 2008. "We Are Ready to Talk to Turkey." *The Wall Street Journal*, July 9.
SOCAR. 2011. "New Era for Azerbaijan's Gas Industry: SOCAR President Rovnag Abdullayev's Interview to ANS TV." *SOCAR*. Accessed April 1, 2013. http://www.socar.az/3892-news-view-en.html/.
Suleymanov, Rashad. 2010. "Azerbaijan and Turkey to Launch Joint Production of Military Equipments Next Year." *APA*, December 8.
Suny, Ronald Grigor. 1996. "On the Road to Independence: Cultural Cohesion and Ethnic Revival in a Multinational Society." In *Transcaucasia, Nationalism, and Social Change: Essays in the History of Armenia, Azerbaijan, and*

Georgia, edited by Ronald Grigor Suny, 377–400. Ann Arbor: The University of Michigan Press.

Tamrazian, Harry. 2000. "Which Formula Can Guarantee Security for the South Caucasus?" *RFE/RL*, June 9.

TASS, "Russia-Azerbaijan Trade Hits $2.6 Billion." 2014. June 23.

Turkish Institute of Statistics. 2015. "Devlet İstatistik Enstitüsü Yıllara Göre Dış Ticaret Verileri." *Turkish Institute of Statistics.* Accessed January 27, 2015. http://www.tuik.gov.tr/PreTablo.do?alt_id=1046/.

Weitz, Richard. 2010. "Russian-Turkish Relations: Steadfast and Changing." *Mediterranean Quarterly* 21(3): 61–85.

3 Low-intensity Turkish–Russian rivalry in the Steppes of Central Asia

Central Asia became another region that witnessed Turkish–Russian competition in the immediate post-Cold War era. The region nowadays, however, has been turning gradually from a region of divergence and competition between Turkey and Russia into one of engagement and cooperation. This transformation stems from the fact that the rivalry here was less severe and vitriolic compared to that in the South Caucasus. Turkey lacked direct access to the region and had less financial, technical and intellectual wherewithal compared to Russia to remedy the needs of the nascent Central Asian republics. Nevertheless, Turkey has been using some political, economic and cultural tools to expand its sphere of influence in Central Asia since the early 1990s to compete with Russia as well as with other players such as Iran and China, but has succeeded most in the economic field so far.

One of the early foreign policy instruments of Turkey toward Central Asia was the foundation of the Turkish Cooperation and Coordination Agency (TİKA) in January 1992. TİKA provided economic, technical, social, cultural and educational cooperation to the Central Asian countries through the establishment of government organizations, preparation of legislation, placement of civil servants, provision of assistance in the areas of banking, insurance, international trade, finance and taxation and deployment of experts.

Another tool Turkey used to position itself as a powerful and effective player in Central Asia has been the convening of Turkic summits since 1992 with the participation of Azerbaijan and Central Asian states of Kazakhstan, Kyrgyzstan, Turkmenistan and Uzbekistan. The idea of creating some kind of a loose Turkic Union with the participation of Azerbaijan and Turkic states had been put forth by the Turkish President Özal who believed that a Turkish Commonwealth similar to the British and French models would strengthen the ties of

Turkey with these countries and boost Turkey's image and position in the region.

The summits acquired an institutional character in October 2009 with the establishment of the Cooperation Council of Turkic Speaking States. The permanent secretariat of the organization is located in İstanbul. The Council has put forth projects for the establishment of a Turkic business council, joint insurance company, transportation administration agency, commission for the harmonization of legislation on property acquisition, development fund, joint arbitration court, Turkic scientific research fund and Turkic inter-university union (Cooperation Council of Turkic Speaking States 2013) to enhance economic and cultural relations by bringing more into line the transportation, legal and education systems of Turkey, Azerbaijan and these four Central Asian states. However, no concrete results have been achieved so far. Furthermore, Uzbekistan's decision not to participate to the Council due to its standoff with Turkey poses a significant obstacle to the success of the organization. Since 1999, the Uzbek government has been accusing Turkey of countenancing the Uzbek opposition, especially Muhammed Salih, the leader of the *Erk* (Freedom) party who lives in exile in Turkey. Uzbek–Turkish relations further got out of order when Turkey voted in favor of two resolutions against Uzbek government that were set forth in Council of the European Union[1] in 2005 and UN in 2006.[2]

The ECO is another regional cooperation mechanism which brings Turkey and Central Asian states together along with Azerbaijan, Iran, Afghanistan and Pakistan. The organization's main purpose is to promote economic, technical and cultural cooperation among the member states. However, intra-regional trade is low and the transit trade and visa simplification agreements have not come into force yet. Cognizant of the lethargy and ineptitude of the organization, Turkey initiated the foundation of the Eminent Persons Group in 2010 to work on projects which will augment the dynamism, visibility and efficiency of the organization (Hazar 2012, 14–5).

Turkey's economic relations with the Central Asian states recorded noticeable progress in the post-Cold War period. The trade volume between Turkey and the Central Asian states which was 146 million dollars in 1992 exceeded nine billion dollars in 2013 and the total investments of Turkish companies in Central Asia came at three and a half billion dollars (Republic of Turkey Ministry of Foreign Affairs 2013). There exist nearly 2,000 Turkish firms mostly operating in energy, construction, retail, textile, consumer goods, tourism and healthcare industries in Central Asia which offer goods and services to

Central Asian consumers as alternative to Chinese and Russian products.

Turkey took steps in educational and cultural matters in Central Asia as well. The Turkish Ministry of National Education and private organizations opened high schools, universities and cultural centers in the region. Turkey also invited students from Central Asian countries to attend Turkish universities by providing them with scholarships. Today, 13,890 Central Asian students receive higher education in Turkish universities (Higher Education Council 2015). Another cultural opening of Turkey to Central Asia became the opening of a new television channel by Turkish Radio and Television Corporation (TRT) in 2009 which broadcasts in Azerbaijani, Kazakh, Kyrgyz, Turkmen and Uzbek languages.

Russia's interest in Central Asia as well as its political, economic and security engagement with the region continued unabated in the post-Cold War period. Different from the South Caucasus, Russia here adopted a regional approach while dealing with the Central Asian affairs and promoted multilateral political, economic and military cooperation under its guidance and leadership through the bodies of Shanghai Cooperation Organization (SCO), EurAsEC, and CSTO.

The SCO, which is composed of Russia and four of five Central Asian states, Kazakhstan, Kyrgyzstan, Tajikistan and Uzbekistan, along with China, was established on June 15, 2001. The organization, to which Turkey was accepted as dialogue partner in June 2012, mostly focuses on promoting regional security and economic cooperation in Eurasia region. With member countries making up three-fifths of the Eurasian landmass and a quarter of the world population (Shanghai Cooperation Organization 2013), the SCO has come out as a serious rival to the Western, especially American, designs in Asia.

The presidents of Russia, Belarus, Kazakhstan, Kyrgyzstan and Tajikistan came together in Astana on October 10, 2000 and founded the EurAsEC. There exists freedom of movement among the member states, and unified tariff preferences system has been in force between Russia, Kazakhstan and Belarus since January 2010 (President of Russia 2009) which transformed into a single economic space in January 2012.[3] With its trade figures exceeding 32 billion dollars in 2013 (Russian Federation Federal State Statistics Service 2015), Russia overtopped Turkey in their economic rivalry in Central Asia, but fell behind China which carried out trade amounting to 50 billion dollars with Central Asia in 2013 (Putz 2015).

The entry of the USA into Central Asia after 9/11, Washington's reaching out to Central Asian states to use their military bases to conduct operations against Taliban forces in Afghanistan and offering military equipment and training to these countries restrained the Russian position in Central Asia by adding another powerful and capable player into Central Asian equation. Russia strove to parry the American influence in the region by reactivating CSTO through the establishment of a Collective Rapid Reaction Force and construction of military bases and the renovation of existing ones. Russia has military bases in Kazakhstan, Kyrgyzstan and Tajikistan and they will continue to constitute important levers for Moscow while vying for influence in the region, especially in the case of a total American pull-out from Afghanistan.

Russian preserves its significance as the major cultural tool of Moscow in Central Asia. Although the language has lost ground in Uzbekistan, Turkmenistan and Tajikistan, Russian is still the lingua franca in Kazakhstan and Kyrgyzstan. Moscow also banks on Russian higher education institutions which provide better education opportunities than the ones in local languages, and various Russian-speaking media channels promote Russian throughout the region (Fierman 2012, 1097–8). Similar to Russia, China is also resorting to elements of soft power in increasing proportions in Central Asia through regular cultural exchanges offering language training and higher education opportunities to the nations of Central Asia. Confucius Institutes have been established in many universities across Central Asia to acquaint the local populations with Chinese language and culture. Lately China has pledged to assist in the training of 1,500 specialists from the SCO countries in the fields of transportation, telecommunications and energy in addition to providing financial support to 30,000 students and professors (Shustov 2012). English is another attractive language in Central Asia, especially for the young generations as it is a significant door-opener for well-paid career opportunities.

The early 1990s witnessed mutual suspicion and resentment on the part of both Ankara and Moscow regarding each other's moves for expansion of influence in Central Asia. While some members of the Turkish Parliament appraised the Russian policy of Near Abroad and the deployment of Russian forces in Tajikistan during the civil war in this country as an extension of Russian tradition of imperialism, Russia approached Turkey's convening of Turkic summits with equal discontent and criticism as denoted by Russian Foreign Ministry spokesman Mikhail Demurin's statement that organization of meetings based on the ethnic bonds would attract aggressive, nationalistic and extremist circles and would bear a certain amount of responsibility for provoking conflicts including in the CIS (Kohen 1994).

The fever of rivalry between Turkey and Russia in Central Asia subsided largely at the beginning of the 2000s following Turkey's acknowledgement that it did not have the requisite political, economic and military potency to overpower Moscow in the region. The official breakthrough came in June 2001 during Russian Minister of Foreign Affairs Ivanov's visit to Turkey. In the course of his meeting with his Russian counterpart, Turkish Foreign Minister Cem suggested the formation of a strategic triangle between Turkey, Russia and Central Asian countries in order to ensure cooperation and consultation pertaining to regional political and economic matters (Çelikpala 2007, 280). Ivanov responded to the offer positively and also pointed out that the time came to broaden the scope of Russian–Turkish interaction and advised Turkish and Russian businessmen to engage in joint projects in the CIS countries (Embassy of the Russian Federation in Turkey 2001). A few months later, in November 2001, the two foreign ministers put their signatures on an Action Plan for Cooperation in Eurasia, the blueprint which crowned the rapprochement between Turkey and Russia.

Russia's embrace of Turkey's offer of compromise in Central Asia stemmed from the fact that Moscow had also come to the conclusion that it was not the undisputed power in Central Asia any more following the corrosive and disruptive impact of the economic crisis of 1998 on Russian economic potential and abroad investments, Washington's entry into Central Asia through military instruments and Beijing's penetration into the region increasingly and vigorously through political, economic and cultural means.

Starting from early 2000s, Turkey set out less ambitious goals in Central Asia compared to the early post-Cold War years and attained more successful results. Turkish policy towards the region has been shaped for the most part according to economic inducements, and Ankara strove to sustain and expand the economic interests and investments of Turkish businessmen in Central Asia. This situation found its most successful reflection in Turkey's ascending economic ties with Kazakhstan and Turkmenistan, two countries which hosted many Turkish firms and Turkish joint-ventures in various sectors of their economies. Uzbekistan became Turkey's third largest trade partner in Central Asia despite the tense and troubled political relations between the two countries.

The main axis of competition between Turkey and Russia in Central Asia remained the struggle for economic primacy in the region. Rivalry in the economic domain, however, did not stop Turkey and Russia from cooperating in the security sphere. The two sides collaborated against international terrorism, especially in the wake of the USA's incursion into Afghanistan after 9/11 through information-sharing and they also worked together to curb human and narcotics trafficking (Weitz 2010, 79).

Turkey's admission to the Chinese and Russian-led SCO which also included four of the five Central Asian countries in June 2012 as a dialogue partner attested to the fact that Turkey's search for enhancing cooperation with two major players in Central Asia found reception on their side as well. The SCO is expected to assume more responsibility in averting non-traditional security threats, especially after the gradual withdrawal of NATO from Afghanistan, and Turkey can make some contribution to the organization in combating terrorism, separatism, narcotics trafficking, human smuggling and illegal immigration (Shanghai Cooperation Organization 2012), taking into consideration its valuable experience and good work within International Security Assistance Force in Afghanistan.

Erdoğan expressed willingness and interest in closer ties with the SCO on more than one occasion ("Turkish PM Erdoğan" 2013) after Turkey's hope of becoming member of the EU faded and the relations came to a dead end because of EU's rejection to open up new chapters necessary for accession due to disagreement over Cyprus. Although Turkey's participation in SCO as a full member seemed to be a distant possibility owing to Ankara's security commitments to NATO, elevating ties with the SCO demonstrates once again Turkey's desire and determination to beef up the Asian dimension of its foreign policy and to come to an understanding with its second and third largest trading partner regarding the Central Asian affairs.

The Black Sea became a region where Turkey and Russia adopted close views, perspectives and policies in the post-Cold War period. Both Moscow and Ankara supported the endurance of the existing status quo in the Black Sea and countered the USA moves to challenge it. The next chapter will delve into the details of this convergence and common outlook between the two countries which is a new and significant phenomenon for the bilateral relationship.

Notes

1 In November 2005, the EU announced a partial suspension of the Partnership and Cooperation Agreement with Uzbekistan on the grounds that the latter refused to sanction an independent inquiry into what happened in Andijan in May 2005. An arms embargo was also put in place, whilst a year-long visa ban had been imposed upon 12 Uzbek officials believed to have played a part in the forcible suppression of the Andijan

demonstrations. "Press Release 2679th Council Meeting General Affairs and External Relations-External Relations," Council of the European Union, accessed April 17, 2013, http://consilium.europa.eu/ueDocs/cms_Data/docs/pressData/en/gena/86441.pdf/.

2 In November 2006, UN Third Committee voted a resolution which condemned Uzbekistan for human rights violations and restrictions on the activities of non-governmental organizations. The resolution was rejected 69 to 74. "Third Committee Takes No Action on Text Concerning Human Rights in Uzbekistan," UN General Assembly, accessed April 17, 2013, http://www.un.org/press/en/2006/gashc3875.doc.htm/.

3 This structure evolved into Eurasian Economic Union on 29 May 2014 after the presidents of Belarus, Kazakhstan and Russia signed the founding treaty.

References

Cooperation Council of Turkic Speaking States. 2013. "Cooperation Council of Turkic Speaking States, Projects." *Cooperation Council of Turkic Speaking States.* Accessed April 17, 2013. http://www.turkkon.org/eng/icerik_multi.php?no=13/.

Çelikpala, Mitat. 2007. "1990'lardan Günümüze Türk-Rus İlişkileri." *Avrasya Dosyası* 13(1): 267–298.

Embassy of the Russian Federation in Turkey. 2001. "Speech by Minister of Foreign Affairs of the Russian Federation Igor Ivanov at Meeting with Representatives of Turkey's Business Circles." *Embassy of the Russian Federation in Turkey.* Accessed April 29, 2013. http://www.turkey.mid.ru/hron/29.html/.

Fierman, William. 2012. "Russian in Post-Soviet Central Asia: A Comparison with the States of the Baltic and South Caucasus." *Europe-Asia Studies* 64 (6): 1077–1100.

Hazar, Numan. 2012. "The Future of the Economic Cooperation Organization (ECO)." *ORSAM Report*, no. 108: 1–55.

Higher Education Council. 2015. "Uyruğa Göre Öğrenci Sayıları Raporu." *Higher Education Council.* Accessed July 12, 2016. https://istatistik.yok.gov.tr/.

Hürriyet Daily News, "Turkish PM Erdoğan to Putin: Take us to Shanghai." 2013. November 22.

Kohen, Sami. 1994. "Turkey, Russia Carve out Power with Oil Routes." *The Christian Science Monitor*, November 23.

President of Russia. 2009. "Dmitry Medvedev Signed the Federal Law on Ratification of the Protocol on a Unified Tariff Preferences System within the Customs Union of Russia, Kazakhstan, and Belarus." *President of Russia.* Accessed April 29, 2013. http://eng.kremlin.ru/text/news/2009/11/223104.shtml/.

Putz, Catherine. 2015. "Will All Roads in Central Asia Eventually Lead to China?" *The Diplomat*, June 9.

Republic of Turkey Ministry of Foreign Affairs. 2013. "Orta Asya Ülkeleri ile İlişkiler." *Republic of Turkey Ministry of Foreign Affairs.* Accessed February 2, 2015. http://www.mfa.gov.tr/turkiye-orta-asya-ulkeleri-iliskileri.tr.mfa/.

Russian Federation Federal State Statistics Service. 2015. "External Trade of the Russian Federation with the CIS Countries." *Russian Federation Federal State Statistics Service.* Accessed July 19, 2016. http://www.gks.ru/bgd/regl/b15_12/IssWWW.exe/stg/d02/27-05.htm/.

Shanghai Cooperation Organization. 2012. "Press Release of the Ministry of Foreign Affairs of Turkey regarding the SCO's Acceptance of Turkey as a Dialogue Partner." *Shanghai Cooperation Organization.* Accessed April 29, 2013. http://www.sectsco.org/EN123/show.asp?id=341/.

Shanghai Cooperation Organization. 2013. "Brief Introduction to the Shanghai Cooperation Organisation." *Shanghai Cooperation Organization.* Accessed April 29, 2013. http://www.sectsco.org/EN123/brief.asp/.

Shustov, Alexander. 2012. "China's Growing Importance to Central Asia." *International Affairs*, June 29.

Weitz, Richard. 2010. "Russian-Turkish Relations: Steadfast and Changing." *Mediterranean Quarterly* 21(3): 61–85.

4 Collaboration in the Black Sea

Starting from the eighteenth century up until the early twentieth century the Black Sea region witnessed a fierce and continuous rivalry between the Ottoman and the Russian Empires which revealed itself in the form of nine battles fought between the two countries for supremacy in the area. The foundation of the Republic of Turkey and the Soviet Union on the ruins of the Ottoman and the Tsarist Empires following the First World War and the signing of the Montreux Convention in 1936 put an end to this long-term competition and commenced an era of peace and stability in the Black Sea.

The Convention, while underlining the sovereignty of Turkey in the Sea of Marmara and the Straits of the Bosporus and the Dardanelles, also granted remarkable privileges to the littoral countries including the Soviet Union over the non-littoral states regarding the tonnage of the war vessels passing through the Straits and their length of stay in the Black Sea (Republic of Turkey Ministry of Foreign Affairs 1936). This legal regime of the Turkish Straits determined by the Montreux Convention remained intact during the Cold War years despite the Soviet leader Stalin's push for revision in the treaty for joint administration and defense of the Straits in the wake of the Second World War (Howard 1947, 47–68).

The preservation of the Montreux Convention in its current structure has been the cornerstone of Turkey's Black Sea strategy in the post-Cold War period amidst suggestions from the new NATO members such as Bulgaria and Romania to stretch out the agreement in order to allow a larger USA and/or NATO presence in the Black Sea (Aydın 2014, 389). From Turkey's point of view the Montreux Convention is invaluable and indispensable as it strikes a delicate balance between its military and security obligations to NATO and its flourishing political and economic engagement with Russia. On the one hand, Turkey's control of the Sea of Marmara and the Straits equips the NATO with military and strategic preponderance vis-à-vis Russia in the Eastern Mediterranean (Simon 2014, 75). On the other hand, explicit advantages granted to littoral states in the Montreux Convention such as having the right to send through the Straits both submarines and battleships of higher tonnage than the non-littoral states as well as the constraints restricting the maneuver capability of the non-littoral states ensured that Russia was at ease with the current status quo in the Black Sea region and did not feel itself vulnerable against the USA.

Turkey's desire to maintain the naval balance set forth in the Black Sea region with the Montreux Convention led her to reach a common understanding with Russia in the post-Cold War era in the form of preserving a common front against the access of extra-regional forces, especially the USA and NATO, into the area. The political, economic and security cooperation between the two countries in the Black Sea is carried out under the auspices of the BSEC which was established in 1992 with Turkey's initiative and the participation of Albania, Armenia, Azerbaijan, Bulgaria, Greece, Georgia, Moldova, Romania, Russia and Ukraine (Black Sea Economic Cooperation Organization 2013a).[1]

Nearly a quarter of a century has passed since the inauguration of the BSEC, yet it is still hard to say if the organization has evolved into an effective and efficient structure. It is possible to number four reasons why the BSEC has not lived up to initial expectations and lagged behind most of its objectives, such as free movement of businessmen, elimination of tariffs and establishment of a BSEC free trade area. First of all, there was the problem of a serious shortage of capital in the Black Sea region. At the inception of the BSEC, all of the member countries except Greece and Turkey were grappling with the issue of transition to a market economy and suffered from a decline in national income coupled with high inflation and unemployment. In the following years, Turkey and Russia, the two countries that were expected to galvanize the organization, encountered two severe financial crises and they were not in a position to supply capital for the financing of the organization, as they too were looking for outside financial assistance in order to recover their ailing economic situations.

Second, there existed significant bilateral political disputes between the member states. Armenia and Azerbaijan sparred over Nagorno-Karabakh, Greece and Turkey over Cyprus and the delimitation of the Aegean Sea, Georgia and Russia over Abkhazia and South Ossetia, Moldova and Russia over Transnistria region, Ukraine and Russia over Crimea and Albania and Serbia over Kosovo. Most of the time it became difficult to find a common denominator as the member states focused on their bilateral issues rather than on the agenda of the organization during the meetings.

Third, the participating states' obligations regarding their membership to other international organizations, particularly to the EU and World Trade Organization, impeded full economic integration on a regional scale. Lastly, the BSEC experienced hurdles resulting from a lack of coherent definition of aims, priorities and long-term issues and low efficiency in implementing adopted resolutions and decisions.[2] In order to cope with these difficulties, the BSEC in recent years has brought forth a project-oriented vision that promoted cooperation through development programs and projects of common interest between BSEC states. In this context, the BSEC speeded up its efforts in the areas of communications, transport and trade and development.

With the Memorandum of Understanding in the field of postal services, the agencies responsible for information technologies and telecommunications of the member states decided to develop cooperation in the areas of information-communication technologies (Black Sea Economic Cooperation Organization 2006). In the transportation area, emphasis was given to the development of the Black Sea Ring Highway and the Motorways of the Sea infrastructure projects as they would constitute regional contributions to the extension of Trans-European networks and the development of Euro-Asian transport links. The Black Sea Ring Highway project envisages a four lane ring highway system, approximately 7,100 km long, to connect the BSEC member states with each other (Black Sea Economic Cooperation Organization 2013b). The project on development of the Motorways of the Sea in the BSEC region aims to strengthen the maritime links among the ports of the participating countries as well as the enhancement of maritime security and safety in the BSEC region. These two assignments will help BSEC to gain visibility and attention in the eyes of the citizens of the BSEC countries as they will make concrete difference in the lives of the people of the region by boosting trade and tourism. Moreover, they will also contribute to people-to-people diplomacy by bringing citizens of the BSEC region closer. In the field of trade and development, member states concentrated on trade facilitation in the forms of elimination of non-tariff barriers and business/investment disincentives, simplification of visa procedures for businessmen and professional drivers and further interaction between the business communities of the BSEC countries.

The BSEC enabled Turkey and Russia to come together within the framework of a multilateral security structure, Black Sea Naval

Cooperation Task Group (BLACKSEAFOR), along with four Black Sea littoral countries: Bulgaria, Georgia, Romania and Ukraine. The idea of setting up a multinational naval peace task force was initiated by Turkey at the second Chiefs of the Black Sea Navies meeting which was held in Varna, Bulgaria in 1998. After three years of talks and negotiations, the founding agreement of BLACKSEAFOR was signed in İstanbul on April 2, 2001 (Black Sea Naval Cooperation Task Group 2013a). The principal duties of the task group would be search and rescue operations, humanitarian assistance, mine countermeasures, environmental protection and goodwill visits (Black Sea Naval Cooperation Task Group 2013b). The BLACKSEAFOR started to conduct joint operations right after its foundation. The first was a search and rescue mission that took place in Turkey and the other was a marine demining activity in Ukraine.

The BLACKSEAFOR political consultation group gatherings and the occasional Black Sea naval commanders meetings provided military officials of Turkey and Russia with the opportunity to get together in multilateral structures. Furthermore, when Turkey launched Operation Black Sea Harmony on March 1, 2004, a mission to randomly patrol the Black Sea, detect and trail ships suspected of being involved in illegal activities, Russia became the first littoral state to participate in this initiative on December 27, 2006.[3]

Turkey and Russia jointly demurred to the American proposal to expand NATO-led Operation Active Endeavor in Mediterranean into the Black Sea.[4] Russia was categorically opposed to the expansion of any NATO activity close to its borders. Turkey's wavering stemmed from the fact that passage of a NATO marine task force through the Turkish Straits could contravene the Montreux Convention. Furthermore, there was not much need to establish a new NATO initiative in the Black Sea while three of the six littoral states were already members of the Alliance. In line with this reasoning both Russia and Turkey pointed out that security and confidence-building measures taken up within the framework of the BSEC would be appropriate and sufficient to parry any kind of hazard and threat in the region (Torbakov 2006).

Turkey found itself between a rock and a hard place while trying to sustain the status quo in the Black Sea region in the times of serious crises such as the war between Georgia and Russia over South Ossetia in 2008 and the conflict between Ukraine and Russia over Crimea in 2014. During those times Turkey walked on thin ice to convince Russia that it was complying by the clauses of the Montreux Convention strictly and carefully while paying extra attention not to alienate the USA that wanted to lend more support to the two long-standing members of the NATO's PfP program in their confrontation with a militarily aggressive and superior Russia.

Designated by the Russian Deputy Chief of General Staff Colonel General Alexander Skvorzov as one of the major guarantors of peace and tranquility in the Black Sea area (Skvorzov 2004), the Montreux Convention is seen by the Russian administration not just as an agreement to abide by but also as a significant leverage to be jealously protected against the encroachments of the geographically remote countries. For this reason even the emergence of a possibility of a slight divergence from the Montreux Convention sufficed to make Russian foreign policy-makers' hair stand on end and to issue warnings to Turkey.

The Russian sensitivity regarding strict adherence to the Montreux regime manifested itself clearly when in the wake of the Russian–Georgian conflict of August 2008; the USA decided to send humanitarian aid to Georgia through its two warships. Originally, Washington intended to dispatch two navy hospitals, the USNS *Comfort* and the USNS *Mercy*, to Georgia but the Turkish side objected to these two vessels as their aggregate weight amounted approximately to 140,000 tons, much higher than the maximum limit of 45,000 tons permitted for non-Black Sea powers in the Montreux Convention (Daly 2008). In the end, three smaller American ships crossed the Turkish Straits to carry relief to Georgia. Furthermore, after a sharp statement coming from the Russian Deputy Chief of General Staff Colonel General Anatoly Nogovitsyn on August 27, 2008, which stated that if the NATO ships did not leave the Black Sea after 21 days in line with the Montreux legal blueprint then Turkey would be deemed responsible (Hacıoğlu 2008), Turkish Ministry of Foreign Affairs felt the need to issue an information note that enumerated the basic principles of passage through Turkish Straits for non-littoral countries (Republic of Turkey Ministry of Foreign Affairs 2008) and Ministry officials confirmed that Turkey would insist on the application of the relevant provisions of the agreement scrupulously ("Türkiye'den Rusya'ya Montrö Güvencesi" 2008).

In April 2014, Turkey again felt the need to declare that it had been implementing the terms of the Montreux Convention regarding the Turkish Straits rigorously since the first inauguration of the agreement (Republic of Turkey Ministry of Foreign Affairs 2014a) and underlined that the Convention contributed significantly to the security of the Black Sea littoral countries (Republic of Turkey Ministry of Foreign Affairs 2014b). This declaration came as a response to the claims of the Russian Foreign Minister Lavrov who stated that the USA warships sent to the Black Sea to provide support to the Ukrainian government in its collusion with Russia over Crimea over-extended their stay there in contravention of the Montreux Convention (Ministry of Foreign Affairs of the Russian Federation 2014).

It was clear that Turkey was not happy with the Russian annexation of Crimea which was formalized after the Russian President Putin's signing of the unification agreement on March 18, 2014. The agreement was hammered out following a controversial referendum held two days earlier to which the Crimean Tatars, kinsmen of Turkey, that made up approximately 10 percent of the population of the peninsula, refused to participate en masse (Shiskin and Troianovski 2014). Turkey had previously declared that the referendum would not contribute to the settlement of the crisis in the country (Republic of Turkey Ministry of Foreign Affairs 2014c). Accordingly, it did not recognize Russian rule in the peninsula and made statements which stressed that Crimea was still part of Ukraine.

Another significant concern for Turkey was the preservation of the political rights and socio-economic well-being of the Tatar population in a Russian-controlled Crimea. Although Russia made Tatar one of the official languages of the administrative region (Özdal 2015), it prevented prominent Crimean leaders such as the former President of the Crimean Tatar National Assembly Mustafa Abdülcemil Kırımoğlu and his successor Refat Çubarov from entering into Crimea for five years (Republic of Turkey Ministry of Foreign Affairs 2014d). Furthermore, ATR, the independent Crimean Tatar television channel took off air in April 2015 after its application to the Russian authorities for license renewal was rejected many times.

The breakdown of Turkish–Russian relations following the November 2015 plane incident led Turkey to denounce these Russian moves in strongly worded press releases. Especially after the prohibition of the activities of the Mejlis of the Crimean Tatar People on April 26, 2016, Turkish Ministry of Foreign Affairs accused Russia of following a systematic policy of suppression and intimidation towards the Crimean Tatars (Republic of Turkey Ministry of Foreign Affairs 2016). Despite high-pitched criticisms directed against Russia, Turkey was aware of the fact that these diatribes fell on deaf ears in Russia at a time of strained relations. Therefore, gradual normalization of Turkish–Russian relations starting from the end of June 2016 might help Ankara and Moscow to find a compromise and ameliorate the political conditions of the Crimean Tatars.

Turkey was also apprehensive of the fact that Russia with the appropriation of Crimea has strengthened its stronghold in the northern part of the Black Sea and expanded its zone of influence further in the region subsequent to the outbreak of the pro-Russian separatist currents in the Eastern Ukraine. However, Ankara saw no benefit in cornering Russia by imposing economic sanctions on the country as this would be detrimental for its own economic interests as well. This rationale was also acknowledged by the Turkish Foreign Minister Mevlüt Çavuşoğlu in an interview given to the German newspaper *Die Zeit* in February 2015. Underlining that Turkey did not have any obligations to join the EU sanctions against Russia, Çavuşoğlu stated that Russia was an important trade partner of Turkey and Turkey would take its own measures if needed (Republic of Turkey Ministry of Foreign Affairs 2015).

Due to its inclusive character of encompassing a broad geography spanning from the Balkans to the South Caucasus and bringing together states in Ankara and Moscow's neighborhood, the BSEC is still promoted as the main regional cooperation scheme in the Black Sea both by Russia and Turkey despite its shortcomings and weaknesses. Moreover, by being in the same organization for nearly a quarter of a century and working towards common goals earned the Russian and Turkish officials and elites the ability to learn which approaches worked better than others vis-à-vis each other. Thus the BSEC overall has a positive impact on Turkish–Russian relationship as a showcase of governmental learning which has increased capabilities of the two states to communicate and reach mutually beneficial agreements (Keohane and Nye 1987, 746). Therefore both of the countries frowned upon the establishment of new regional structures in the Black Sea spearheaded by other littoral states such as Georgia, Ukraine and Romania and backed up by the USA that could function as potential rivals to the BSEC. In this context, the new regional cooperation organizations such as The Community of Democratic Choice (CDC) and the Black Sea Forum for Partnership and Dialogue (BSFPD) received a tepid welcome from Turkey and Russia. Both countries were represented at low levels at these platforms and Turkish and Russian attendees of these associations designated BSEC as the actual rostrum for the solution of regional matters.

On August 12, 2005, Georgian President Saakashvili and his Ukrainian counterpart Viktor Yuschenko met at the Georgian town of Borjomi and hammered out the Borjomi Declaration which invited the countries of the post-Soviet space to join them in a new coalition which would aim at promoting democracy and security in the area stretching from the Baltics to the Caspian Sea (Chauffour 2005). The CDC was set up in Kiev on December 2, 2005, in the presence of Presidents of Estonia, Georgia, Latvia, Lithuania, Macedonia, Moldova, Romania, Slovenia and Ukraine, along with government delegations from Azerbaijan, Bulgaria, Czech Republic, Hungary, Poland, Slovakia as well as observers from the EU, the USA, and the OSCE. The organization was founded as a governmental and non-governmental forum of cooperation for dialogue, through which the participating states proclaimed to cooperate closely towards achieving the common goal of establishing lasting peace, democracy, economic and social development in addition to combating against corruption, money laundering, organized crime, terrorism and illicit trafficking in arms, drugs and human beings (National Security Council of Georgia 2005). The Russian government which characterized the formation as a pro-American design intended to curb and weaken Russian influence in the Black Sea sent an embassy official to the inauguration, whereas Turkey also demonstrated a minimal presence in the meeting by sending a junior official from the Foreign Ministry (Vorotnyuk 2006).

On June 5, 2006, Bucharest hosted a summit launching the BSFPD with the addition of the presidents of Romania, Moldova, Ukraine, Georgia, Armenia and Azerbaijan, plus the attendance of ministers from Bulgaria, Greece, and Turkey and a senior official from the USA as observers. According to the Joint Declaration released at the end of the gathering, the forum, which would have no permanent structures or bodies, would serve as a regional platform to endorse good governance, identify regional means and capabilities that could be mobilized to guarantee sustainable development and encourage cooperation in the fields of crisis management, civil emergency planning, post-conflict reconstruction and environmental protection (Black Sea Forum for Partnership and Dialogue 2006).

Russia authorized its ambassador to Romania, Nikolai Tolkachev, to sit in the meeting as an observer. Tolkachev conveyed the official Russian position in the course of the summit, which saw the existing cooperation frameworks such as the BSEC and BLACKSEAFOR as adequate mechanisms for deepening regional cooperation in the Black Sea (Socor 2006). Turkish Minister of State Beşir Atalay in a similar vein avowed that the Romanian initiative would not dilute the importance of the BSEC, which remained the actual platform for the procurement of solutions to the problems of the region ("Ankara: Black Sea Partnership" 2006). A representative from the Turkish Ministry of Foreign Affairs also acknowledged that Turkey's part in the forum was about seeing what was going on in a newly created rival regional organization rather than having the interest and will to become a genuine partner of it (Meltem Atay, Executive Manager of the BSEC, interview with the author, November 20, 2008).

Turkey and Russia, with their geographical location, historical experience and growing economic power, are the driving forces that can spur the BSEC further towards success. However, they should strive more for concrete joint projects and programs and motivate the other member states more willingly and whole-heartedly for closer regional cooperation.

The next chapter will examine the impact of separatist Chechen and Kurdish movements on Turkish–Russian relations. These two movements, due to their direct and vehement attack on the unity and territorial integrity of Russia and Turkey, had cast a long shadow on the Turkish–Russian interaction for most of the 1990s. Although both Ankara and Moscow are still far away from bringing out a palatable and permanent solution to these two poignant issues, their negative influence on the overall Turkish–Russian relationship waned in the early 2000s concomitant to the elevating economic and political ties between the two countries.

Notes

1 Serbia and Montenegro was granted BSEC membership status in April 2004 and it was inherited by Serbia after the Federation of Serbia and Montenegro was dissolved in May 2006.
2 The BSEC, at its early foundation, also suffered from lack of a serious, powerful and effective secretariat. Excessive bureaucratic procedures and red tape on the part of the Turkish side further impeded the functioning of the organization. Ambassador Murat Sungar, First Deputy Secretary General of the BSEC, interview with the author, November 20, 2008.
3 Ukraine joined Black Sea Harmony on January 17, 2007 and Romania was included in the structure on December 6, 2010. See "Operation Black Sea Harmony (OBSH)," Turkish Naval Forces, accessed May 26, 2013, https://www.dzkk.tsk.tr/icerik.php?dil=0&icerik_id=27/.
4 Operation Active Endeavor was constituted in late 2001 following the terrorist attacks against the USA on September 11. Its mission is to conduct maritime operations in the Mediterranean zone against terrorism, illicit arms and drug trafficking, and illegal immigration. See "Operation Active Endeavor," Allied Maritime Component Command Naples, accessed May 26, 2013, http://www.afsouth.nato.int/JFCN_Operations/ActiveEndeavour/Endeavour.htm/.

References

Anatolian Times, "Ankara: Blacksea Partnership & Dialogue Forum Starts." 2006. June 6.

Aydın, Mustafa. 2014. "Turkish Policy towards the Wider Black Sea and the EU Connection." *Journal of Balkan and Near Eastern Studies* 16(3): 383–397.

Black Sea Economic Cooperation Organization. 2006. "Memorandum of Understanding on Multilateral Cooperation in the Field of Postal Service." *Black Sea Economic Cooperation Organization*. Accessed May 26, 2013. http://www.bsec-organization.org/admin/Annex percent20II percent20- percent20MoU percent20PostalService.pdf/.

Black Sea Economic Cooperation Organization. 2013a. "BSEC at a glance." *Black Sea Economic Cooperation Organization*. Accessed May 26, 2013. http://www.bsec-organization.org/Information/Pages/bsec.aspx/.

Black Sea Economic Cooperation Organization. 2013b. "Areas of Cooperation, Transport, Information." *Black Sea Economic Cooperation Organization*. Accessed May 26, 2013. http://www.bsec-organization.org/aoc/Transport/Pages/Information.aspx/.

Black Sea Forum for Partnership and Dialogue. 2006. "Joint Declaration of the Black Sea Forum for Dialogue and Partnership." *Black Sea Forum for Partnership and Dialogue*. Accessed May 26, 2013. http://www.blackseaforum.org/joint_declaration.html/.

Black Sea Naval Cooperation Task Group. 2013a. "BLACKSEAFOR Chronology." *Black Sea Naval Cooperation Task Group*. Accessed May 26, 2013. http://www.blackseafor.org/English/Chronology_Home.asp/.

Black Sea Naval Cooperation Task Group. 2013b. "BLACKSEAFOR Agreement." *Black Sea Naval Cooperation Task Group*. Accessed May 26, 2013. http://www.blackseafor.org/English/Agreement_Home.asp/.

Chauffour, Célia. 2005. "Ongoing Special: The Community of Democratic Choice, the Stakes of a Remarkable Diplomatic Feat." *Caucaz Europe News*, November 4.

Daly, John C.K. 2008. "Turkey Pursues its Own Foreign Policy Line." *Eurasia Daily Monitor* 5(207), October 29.

Hacıoğlu, Nerdun. 2008. "Montrö Faturası." *Hürriyet*, August 28.

Howard, Harry N. 1947. *The Problem of the Turkish Straits*. Washington: United States Government Printing Office.

Hürriyet. "Türkiye'den Rusya'ya Montrö Güvencesi." 2008. August 27.

Keohane, Robert O., and Joseph S. Nye. 1987. "Power and Interdependence Revisited." *International Organization* 41(4): 725–753.

Ministry of Foreign Affairs of the Russian Federation. 2014. "Speech by the Russian Foreign Minister Sergey Lavrov and His Answers to Questions from the Mass Media during Joint Press Conference Summarizing the Results of Negotiations with the Minister of Foreign Affairs of Kazakhstan, Erlan Idrisov." *Ministry of Foreign Affairs of the Russian Federation*. Accessed

Collaboration in the Black Sea 75

May 2, 2014. http://www.mid.ru/bdomp/brp_4.nsf/e78a48070f128a
7b43256999005bcbb3/2413dda17a0a2d7544257cb0005296f1!/.
National Security Council of Georgia. 2005. "Declaration of the Countries of the Community of Democratic Choice." *National Security Council of Georgia.* Accessed May 26, 2013. http://www.nsc.gov.ge/download/pdf/decl/EN. pdf/.
Özdal, Habibe. 2015. "The Influence of the Ukraine Crisis on Turkish-Russian Relations." *USAK,* March 11.
Republic of Turkey Ministry of Foreign Affairs. 1936. "Boğazlar Rejimi Hakkında Montreux'de 20 Temmuz 1936 Tarihinde İmza Edilen Mukavelename." *Republic of Turkey Ministry of Foreign Affairs.* Accessed May 21, 2015. http://ua.mfa.gov.tr/.
Republic of Turkey Ministry of Foreign Affairs. 2008. "Montrö Sözleşmesi Uygulamaları Hakkında Özet Not." *Republic of Turkey Ministry of Foreign Affairs.* Accessed May 26, 2013. http://www.mfa.gov.tr/bn_11—23-a gustos-2008_-montro-sozlesmesi-uygulamalari-hakkinda-ozet-not.tr.mfa/.
Republic of Turkey Ministry of Foreign Affairs. 2014a. "Statement of the Spokesman of the Ministry of Foreign Affairs of Turkey in response to a Question Regarding the Statements of Russian Foreign Minister on the Montreux Convention ." *Republic of Turkey Ministry of Foreign Affairs.* Accessed May 2, 2014. http://www.mfa.gov.tr/qa_5_-3-april-2014_-statem ent-of-the-spokesman-of-the-ministry-of-foreign-affairs-of-turkey-in-resp onse-to-a-question-regardin.en.mfa/.
Republic of Turkey Ministry of Foreign Affairs. 2014b. "Press Release Regarding the Implementation of the Montreux Convention." *Republic of Turkey Ministry of Foreign Affairs.* Accessed May 2, 2014. http://www.mfa. gov.tr/no_-116_-12-april-2014_-press-release-regarding-the-implementatio n-of-the-montreux-convention.en.mfa/.
Republic of Turkey Ministry of Foreign Affairs. 2014c. "Press Release Regarding the Latest Developments in Crimea." *Republic of Turkey Ministry of Foreign Affairs.* Accessed May 22, 2015. http://www.mfa.gov.tr/no_ -77_-6-march-2014_-press-release-regarding-the-latest-developments-in-crim ea.en.mfa/.
Republic of Turkey Ministry of Foreign Affairs. 2014d. "Press Release Regarding the Mounting Pressure and Unlawful Practices against the Crimean Tatar National Assembly and the Crimean Tatars." *Republic of Turkey Ministry of Foreign Affairs.* Accessed May 22, 2015. http://www.mfa. gov.tr/no_-231_-7-july-2014_-press-release-regarding-the-mounting-p ressure-and-unlawful-practices-against-the-crimean-tatar-national-assem bly-and-the-crimean-tatars.en.mfa/.
Republic of Turkey Ministry of Foreign Affairs. 2015. "Dışişleri Bakanı Sayın Mevlüt Çavuşoğlu'nun Die Zeit Gazetesine Verdiği Özel Mülakat." *Republic of Turkey Ministry of Foreign Affairs.* Accessed May 22, 2015. http://www. mfa.gov.tr/disisleri-bakani-sayin-mevlut-cavusoglu_nun-die-zeit-gazetesine-vermis-olduklari-mulakat_-12-subat-2015.tr.mfa/.

Republic of Turkey Ministry of Foreign Affairs. 2016. "Press Release Regarding the Prohibition of the Activities of the Mejlis of the Crimean Tatar People." *Republic of Turkey Ministry of Foreign Affairs.* Accessed July 21, 2016. http://www.mfa.gov.tr/no_-102_-27-april-2016_-press-release-rega rding-the-prohibition-of-the-activities-of-the-mejlis-of-the-crimean-tatar-p eople.en.mfa/.

Shiskin, Philip, and Anton Troianovski. 2014. "Crimean Tatars Appear to Boycott Voting: Many Deeply Suspicious of Russian Intentions." *The Wall Street Journal*, March 17.

Simon, Luis. 2014. "NATO's Rebirth: Assessing NATO's Eastern European Flank." *Parameters* 43(3): 67–79.

Skvorzov, Alexander. 2004. "Black Sea Security: The Russian Viewpoint." Paper presented at the annual meeting for the Center for Strategic Decision Research, Berlin, May 7–10.

Socor, Vladimir. 2006. "Moscow, Ankara Reluctant to Welcome New Black Sea Forum." *Eurasia Daily Monitor* 3(112), June 9.

Torbakov, Igor. 2006. "Turkey Sides with Moscow against Washington on Black Sea Force." *Eurasia Daily Monitor* 3(43), March 3.

Vorotnyuk, Maryna 2006. "Turkey's Attitude toward the Community of Democratic Choice." Accessed May 26, 2013. http://www.niss.od.ua/p/130. doc/.

5 Sensitive spots: Chechen and Kurdish matters

Chechnya became part of the Tsarist Russian empire in the nineteenth century after the result of a long, fierce and wearisome battle. The Chechen territory was merged with Ingushetia during the Soviet time and the Chechen–Ingush Autonomous Soviet Socialist Republic was declared on December 5, 1936 (Gammer 2006, 152). The elections which took place in October 1991, just before the demise of the Soviet Union, brought to power in the Chechen–Ingush Republic Dzhokhar Dudayev, a former general in the Soviet Air Force.

On November 2, 1991, Dudayev announced the establishment of an independent and sovereign Chechen Republic of Ichkeria, a decision which was repudiated immediately both by Moscow and the Ingush administration.[1] Russia resorted to a full-scale military assault in December 1994 after its attempts to overthrow Dudayev came to naught. The war which lasted nearly two years, much to the consternation and disillusionment of Russian government, ended in August 1996 with the signing of Khasavyurt Agreement. The agreement encapsulated the withdrawal of Russian forces from Chechnya, Russian rebuilding of the socio-economic infrastructure of the Chechen Republic, reconstruction of mutual budgetary, currency and fiscal relations between the parties and the supply of food and medical aid to the population (Gammer 2006, 221–3). Although the future status of Chechnya was not mentioned in the document, the acceptance of Russia entering into a truce agreement with one of its rebellious autonomous republics and the inclusion of the right of self-determination in the text was a remarkable feat for the Chechens.

Russia could not let Chechnya leave the federation, as the secession of the Chechen Republic could incite separatist tendencies in other provinces of Russia. In addition, the Baku-Novorossiysk pipeline, which carried Azeri oil to the Russian Black Sea ports, passed through Chechen territory. Lastly, Chechnya shared a border with the South

Ossetia region of Georgia, a province that had cordial relations with Russia and which Russia used as leverage against the Georgian state.

Chechnya came to the attention of Turkey when Shamil Basayev hijacked an Aeroflot jet with its 178 passengers and re-routed it to Ankara on November 9, 1991. Basayev claimed that his was a protest act to impel the international community to take notice of the Russian troop deployment in Chechen territory (Smith 2006, 127). After five hours of circling in the air, the plane returned to Grozny and the hostages were released. In January 1996, six Turkish citizens of Abkhaz and Chechen origin, along with an Abkhaz and two Chechens, kidnapped the *Avrasya* ferry which was getting ready to travel to Sochi from the Turkish Black Sea port of Trabzon ("Türkiye Eylem Sahası" 2002). The militants demanded that Russia allow the departure of Chechen fighters from Pervamoiskoye where they were under attack from Russian heavy artillery and helicopter gunships as a result of their raid on the Russian military airbase in Kizlyar, Dagestan and taking 160 civilians hostage (Lieven 1998, 139). The ferryboat incident ended three days later after the surrender of the hijackers. In the wake of the crisis, while Russian President Boris Yeltsin sent a note of thanks to his Turkish counterpart Demirel for Turkey's cooperation in solving the hijacking incident, he also suggested in his note that Turkey and Russia should cooperate in their shared uncompromising stand against terror ("Russia Seeks" 1996). Moscow also openly conveyed its annoyance and disappointment to Turkish authorities in February 1997 when the İstanbul State Security Court decided to try the hijacking case as interference in the ferry's direction rather than as a terrorist act (Mollaoğlu 1997).

For the Turkish government, the Chechen issue was an internal matter for Russia, to be resolved within the confines of the territorial integrity of the Russian Federation and without losing emphasis on respect for human rights. However, Turkey also sheltered citizens of Chechen descent who had immigrated to the Ottoman empire following the Russian conquest of the North Caucasus and they supported their kindred with rallies and financial aid.

Russia saw Turkey as an intruder who, through its Chechen and Caucasian diaspora, interfered in the affairs of Russia with the objective of debilitating the Russian state and gaining supremacy in the Caucasus and Central Asia. Dudayev's visits to Turkey and his reception by the Prime Minister Demirel were criticized by the Russian officials and Russia also accused Turkey of sending arms and volunteer fighters to the Chechen Republic ("Rusya: Türkiye Çeçenistan'a" 1995).

Russia retaliated to Chechen sympathy in Turkey by permitting the convening of conferences and congresses which were organized by the Kurdish National Liberation Front (ERNK), the political wing of PKK and opening up a Kurdish House in Moscow. Although the Russian government and Ministry of Foreign Affairs rejected any kind of connection with PKK, some members of the Russian Duma attended the conferences hosted by PKK and gave their backing to the Kurdish cause.

Russia and Turkey signed a Protocol to Prevent Terrorism during Turkey's Minister of Interior Nahit Menteşe's visit to his interlocutor Victor Yerin on January 24, 1995. According to the protocol, the two countries would prevent sheltering terrorist organizations in their territories (*Ayın Tarihi*, January 24, 1995). This was followed by the Memorandum on Cooperation against Terrorism on December 18, 1996 in the course of Turkish Minister of Foreign Affairs Tansu Çiller's meeting with Yevgeny Primakov, Russia's foreign minister. The two countries pledged to cooperate against terrorism through prevention of terrorist acts, information exchange and detention of criminals (Republic of Turkey Ministry of Foreign Affairs 1996).

In spite of the agreements Russia did not add PKK to the list of terror groups and the PKK separatists arranged a Conference on Cooperation between Russian and Kurdish People in February 1997. The conference was attended by a number of Duma deputies (*Sabah*, February 14, 1997). Moreover, despite the closure of the Kurdish House, a PKK-controlled training camp was set up in Yaroslavl, lying 250 kilometres northwest of Moscow where the wounded militants were treated and an ideological education was given to the PKK members (Olson 1998, 220). The PKK leader Abdullah Öcalan stayed in Moscow in October–November 1998 before he flew to Italy. Although the Duma passed a resolution pushing Yeltsin for granting Öcalan political asylum, the Russian government avoided such an act which which would strain relations with Turkey (Sezer 2000, 106).

On August 7, 1999, Chechen militants led by Shamil Basayev and Emir Khattab launched an attack in the mountainous Botlikh region in Dagestan, took control of two villages and proclaimed the Islamic Republic of Dagestan on August 10 (German 2003, 151). This was followed by a series of bombings in apartments in Moscow that were attributed to Chechens, although there was not much evidence to support it. As a result of the bomb attacks 294 people were killed (Smith 2006, 26) and this incident paved the way for Russia's second military incursion to Chechnya.

Turkish Prime Minister Bülent Ecevit paid an official visit to Moscow in November 1999 during Russia's second campaign against Chechnya. A joint declaration on cooperation in the fight against terrorism was announced and Ecevit portrayed the Chechen conflict as an internal affair for Russia, a statement which pleased Russian officials but brought on a great deal of criticism from Islamist and nationalist political circles in Turkey.

Turkey continued to provide humanitarian relief to the Chechen people during the Second Russian-Chechen War. Chechens wounded in combat with Russian soldiers were brought to Turkish hospitals (Morris 2000). Some Chechen civilians were lodged in guesthouses in Fenerbahçe, Ümraniye and Beykoz (Taştekin 2001) but these activities were low-profile compared to the first war.

Sporadic hostage incidents brought the Chechen issue to the attention of Turkish public. In March 2001, a plane which flew from İstanbul to Moscow was hijacked and diverted to Medina. The hijackers demanded an end to the war in Chechnya. After a security operation executed by Saudi security forces, a Russian flight attendant, a Turkish passenger and one of the hijackers died ("Operasyon'da Biri Türk" 2001). In April 2001, 13 gunmen burst into the lobby of the Swissotel in İstanbul, took about 120 guests hostage and stated that their action was in protest at Russia's bloody attacks in the Caucasus ("Hostage Drama in Istanbul" 2001). The event was directed by Muhammed Emin Tokcan, who had been the leader of the *Avrasya* ferry hijacking incident in 1996. He had been sentenced to eight years in March 1997 but escaped from prison in October that same year. He was recaptured in 1999 but released from prison in November 2000 under a general amnesty ("Profile: Istanbul Gang's Leader" 2001). Tokcan again surrendered to the Turkish security forces and was sentenced to 12 years imprisonment on December 30, 2002 for his involvement in the hostage-taking act.

The last Chechen hostage incident in Turkey occurred in May 2002 when an armed Turkish citizen held hostage about 13 people at the Marmara Hotel in İstanbul in order to protest at Russia's intervention in Chechnya ("The Marmara'da Rehine Krizi" 2002). The incident ended with the gunman's surrender to the Turkish police.

The Reasons for Turkey's Changing Attitude towards the Chechen Cause

Turkey began to distance itself from the Chechen cause starting with the end of the Second Russian-Chechen War for several reasons. First of all, flourishing Wahhabi ideology in Chechnya, the adoption of Sharia law in the country and the targeting of civilians in terrorist operations estranged both the Turkish administration and the public.

Second, Turkey signed in December 2001 and ratified in January 2002 the UN Convention for the Suppression of the Financing of Terrorism (Commission of the European Communities 2002, 117) and signed in May 2003 (Commission of the European Communities 2003, 113) and ratified in January 2005 (European Commission 2005, 113) the Protocol Amending the European Convention on the Suppression of Terrorism in line with the international campaign on the fight against terrorism which rose to prominence immediately after the terrorist attacks against the USA in September 2011. The signing of the convention and the protocol led Turkish authorities to become more alert regarding the freezing and confiscation of terrorist assets and ensuring that non-profit organizations would not be used to finance terrorist activities. This new situation led to the curtailment of the activities of the Chechen diaspora organizations in Turkey. The Turkish government expropriated 1 million dollars of Caucasus-Chechen Solidarity Committee, and the International Chechen Conference which would be held in İstanbul in May 2002 was cancelled ("Dünya Çeçen" 2002). Furthermore, in November 2002, following the Dubrovka Theater hostage incident,[2] Turkish authorities decided to ban the entry of Chechen leaders such as Mevladi Udugov and Ruslan Gelayev into Turkey and also expelled the so-called representatives of the Chechen Republic of Ichkeria, Badrudin Zelimkhan Arslangereyev and Rakhman Dushuyev from the country (Embassy of the Russian Federation in Turkey 2002).

Lastly and most importantly, deepening economic ties with Russia in the form of increasing bilateral trade and construction of the Blue Stream gas pipeline coupled with the prospect of a thaw in political association urged Turkey to exercise restraint while backing up the Chechen cause. Moscow's overtures to Ankara for better political relations from the highest echelons of the Russian state in the early 2000s contributed greatly to the change of mind of Turkish authorities pertaining to the Chechen matter. The Russian Prime Minister Mikhail Kasyanov who reciprocated Ecevit's visit in October 2000 with a large delegation of Russian ministers declared that "cooperation, not confrontation, was the centerpiece of Russian policy toward Turkey" (*Russian History Encyclopedia* 2013), whereas Russian Minister of Foreign Affairs Ivanov who paid an official visit to Turkey in June 2001 avowed that the extensive field of common interests in different regions, the unprecedentedly high level of trade and economic cooperation and contacts between people dictated taking the relationship to a qualitatively new level (Embassy of the Russian Federation in Turkey 2001a) which he defined as genuine partnership (Embassy of the Russian Federation in Turkey 2001b).

Ankara also developed its ties with the current pro-Russian administration in Chechnya. The President of Chechnya Ramzan Kadyrov accompanied Russian President Medvedev in his visit to Turkey in May 2010 and Turkish Minister of National Defense İsmet Yılmaz, along with the governor and mayor of Sivas, participated in April 2012 in the opening ceremony of a pro-Russian-Chechen association in the city of Sivas ("Yılmaz: Grozni" 2012). This act of the minister, however, was criticized by some of the Chechen solidarity organizations in Turkey (Özer 2012) as it came a couple of months after three militants of the Chechen separatist movement had been killed in İstanbul by weapons used by Russian special forces.[3]

The dissension over Syria exacerbated by Turkey's shooting down of the Russian bomber precipitated Ankara and Moscow to hit each other's soft belly for some time. While Russia claimed that members of the terrorist organizations that were fighting against Russian security units in the North Caucasus were receiving protection and treatment from Turkey (President of Russia 2015), Turkey claimed that Russia provided weapons to the PKK (Garnelis 2016). Furthermore, Turkey resented Russia's allowing the Democratic Union Party (PYD), the Syrian branch of PKK, to open a representative office in Moscow.

The reinstatement of Turkish–Russian ties is expected to act again as a constraining factor in the event of Turkey's and Russia's use of Chechen and Kurdish issues as trump cards to weaken each other. However, it is well-known that both Turkey and Russia are still at pains to contain Chechen and Kurdish separatist currents on their territories. Russia managed to establish a relative peace in Chechnya after making a deal with Kadyrov, and granted him the presidency of Chechnya along with generous funds from the federal budget in exchange of his loyalty to Moscow. However, this move did not prevent the unrest spreading to other North Caucasian republics such as Dagestan, Ingushetia, Kabardino-Balkaria and Karachaevo-Cherkessia. The Turkish government, on the other hand, was looking for reconciliation with the separatist Kurdish movement by incorporating its leader Öcalan into the so-called peace process which was expected to broaden the rights of the Kurdish population in the country. However, the process nose-dived after the renewal of military conflict between PKK and the Turkish security forces in July 2015. For the time being, the future of the peace process in Turkey seemed to be bleak, as evinced by government's resort to military methods to contain Kurdish separatism.

The final chapter of the Part II will focus on a relatively new element in the post-Cold War Turkish–Russian equation, the bilateral interaction in the Middle East. The chapter will investigate the points of convergence and divergence between Turkey and Russia pertaining to the political developments that took place in Tunisia, Egypt, Libya and Syria following the popular uprisings against the long-standing authoritarian administrations in these countries.

Notes

1 Ingushetia joined Russia in 1992 after a referendum held on November 30 – December 1, 1991 in which 92 percent of the population voted for autonomy within the Russian Federation. See Edward Kline, "ASF Chechnya Brief," accessed June 9, 2013, http://asf.wdn.com/cgi/ASFdbs.pl?&action= Linkview&pass=&link_name=doc&link_type_doc=file&main_page=http://a sf.wdn.com/&main_page_title=ASF+Home+Page&layout=noframe&data base=asfdocs_chechbp_num_sprivat&link_res_doc=bp2.898547617.html.
2 Forty-one armed Chechen militants led by Movsar Barayev raided the Dubrovka Theater in Moscow on 23 October 2002 and held 850 people as hostages. They demanded the withdrawal of Russian forces from Chechen territory and the end of the Second Russian-Chechen War. The hijacking crisis ended with the pumping of an unknown chemical gas by the Russian security forces. It killed 39 of the militants as well as 129 of the hostages.
3 Since 2008 six Chechen militants who had been active members of the separatist movement in Chechnya had been killed in İstanbul. While the Russian authorities denied any involvement in the killings, both the Turkish government and the Turkish National Police kept their silence on the matter. See "3 Çeçen'e Suikast Rus Gizli Servisinin 'İntikam Operasyonu'", *Vatan*, September 23, 2011.

References

Ajans Kafkas, "Dünya Çeçen Konferansı'nın İptaline Tepki." 2002. May 18.
BBC News, "Hostage Drama in Istanbul." 2001. April 23.
BBC News, "Profile: Istanbul Gang's Leader." 2001. April 23.
Commission of the European Communities. 2002. *2002 Regular Report on Turkey's Progress towards Accession. Commission of the European Communities*. Accessed July 22, 2016. http://ec.europa.eu/enlargement/archives/pdf/key_documents/2002/tu_en.pdf/.
Commission of the European Communities. 2003. *2003 Regular Report on Turkey's Progress towards Accession. Commission of the European Communities*. Accessed July 22, 2016. http://ec.europa.eu/enlargement/archives/pdf/key_documents/2003/rr_tk_final_en.pdf/.

Embassy of the Russian Federation in Turkey. 2001a. "Transcript of Minister of Foreign Affairs of the Russian Federation Igor Ivanov's Remarks at Joint Press Conference on Results of Talks with Turkish Minister of Foreign Affairs Ismail Cem." *Embassy of the Russian Federation in Turkey.* Accessed June 9, 2013. http://www.turkey.mid.ru/hron/9.html/.

Embassy of the Russian Federation in Turkey. 2001b. "Speech by Minister of Foreign Affairs of the Russian Federation Igor Ivanov at Meeting with Representatives of Turkey's Business Circles." *Embassy of the Russian Federation in Turkey.* Accessed June 9, 2013. http://www.turkey.mid.ru/hron/29.html/.

Embassy of the Russian Federation in Turkey. 2002. "Statement by Alexander Yakovenko, the Official Spokesman of Russia's Ministry of Foreign Affairs Regarding Decision by Turkish Authorities to Ban Entry into Country of Leaders of Terrorist Formations Operating in Chechnya." *Embassy of the Russian Federation in Turkey.* Accessed June 9, 2013. http://www.turkey.mid.ru/hron/20.html.

European Commission. 2005. *Turkey 2005 Progress Report. European Commission.* Accessed July 22, 2016. http://ec.europa.eu/enlargement/archives/pdf/key_documents/2005/package/sec_1426_final_progress_report_tr_en.pdf/.

Gammer, Moshe. 2006. *The Lone Wolf and the Bear: Three Centuries of Chechen Defiance of Russian Rule.* Pittsburgh: University of Pittsburgh Press.

Garnelis, Natalya. 2016. "Moscow Dismisses Claims Russia Supplies Weapons to Kurdistan Workers' Party." *TASS,* June 2.

German, Tracey C. 2003. *Russia's Chechen War.* New York: RoutledgeCurzon.

Hürriyet, "Russia Seeks Anti-Terror Cooperation with Turkey." 1996. January 22.

Hürriyet, "Operasyon'da Biri Türk Üç Ölü Bir Türk Yaralı." 2001. March 16.

Hürriyet, "The Marmara'da Rehine Krizi." 2002. May 4.

Lieven, Anatol. 1998. *Chechnya: Tombstone of Russian Power.* New Haven: Yale University Press.

Milliyet, "Rusya: Türkiye Çeçenistan'a Silah Yolluyor." 1995. October 18.

Mollaoğlu, Jülide. 1997. "Kuznetsov on Avrasya Trial, Weapons Sales." *RFE/RL,* February 28.

Morris, Chris. 2000. "Turkey Succours Wounded Chechens." *BBC News,* February 2.

Olson, Robert. 1998. "Turkish and Russian Foreign Policies, 1991–1997: The Kurdish and Chechnya Questions." *Journal of Muslim Minority Affairs* 18 (2): 209–227.

Özer, Murat. 2012. "Türkiye Rus İşbirlikçisi İmajını Hak Etmiyor." *İMKANDER.* Accessed June 9, 2013. http://www.imkander.org.tr/?aType=haber&ArticleID=258/. *President of Russia.* 2015. "Press Statement and Answers to Journalists' Questions."

President of Russia. 2015. "Press Statement and Answers to Journalists' Questions." Accessed July 24, 2016. http://en.kremlin.ru/events/president/news/50851.

Radikal, "Türkiye Eylem Sahası." 2002. May 7.

Republic of Turkey Ministry of Foreign Affairs. 1996. "Türkiye Cumhuriyeti Hükümeti ile Rusya Federasyonu Hükümeti Arasında Terörizm ile Mücadele Alanında İşbirliğine İlişkin Memorandum ." *Republic of Turkey Ministry of Foreign Affairs.* Accessed June 9, 2013. http://www.mfa.gov.tr/mfa_tr/PDF_Pool/showUAFile.aspx/.

Russian History Encyclopedia. 2013. "Relations with Turkey." Accessed June 9, 2013. http://www.answers.com/topic/relations-with-turkey/.

Sezer, Duygu Bazoğlu. 2000. "Turkish-Russian Relations: From Adversity to Virtual Rapprochement." In *Turkey's New World: Changing Dynamics in Turkish Foreign Policy*, edited by Alan Makovsky and Sabri Sayarı, 92–115. Washington: The Washington Institute for Near East Policy.

Smith, Sebastian. 2006. *Allah's Mountains: The Battle for Chechnya.* New York: Tauris Parke Paperbacks.

Taştekin, Fehim. 2001. "Çeçen Mülteci Sorunu." *Kafkas Foundation.* Accessed June 9, 2013. http://www.kafkas.org.tr/ajans/Cecen_Multeci_Sorunu.htm/.

Timetürk, "Yılmaz: Grozni Bir Daha Yıkılmasın." 2012. April 8.

6 The growing gap in the Middle East

The Middle East has become an important item in the foreign policy agendas of both Turkey and Russia since the early 2000s. The invasion of Iraq by a coalition spearheaded by the USA, the remarkable progress Iran recorded in its nuclear program, the sporadic conflagration of the Israeli–Palestinian conflict and finally the outburst of the popular uprisings against the repressive and undemocratic regimes in Tunisia, Egypt, Libya, Bahrain, Yemen and Syria have all aroused both Ankara's and Moscow's interest in and engagement with the region.

Turkey and Russia had demonstrated similar stances with respect to many Middle Eastern matters until the eruption of the conflict in Syria in the spring of 2011. Both of them opposed the American-led military action against Iraq. Turkey's objection proved to be pretty significant as the Turkish Parliament rejected a motion in March 2003 to allow the USA to open the second front from the north of Iraq, which would thus facilitate the occupation of the country by US troops. Ankara and Moscow resisted for a long time Western calls to cast out Iran and Syria as evil or rogue states and instead recommended political dialogue and negotiation to re-engage these two countries into the international system. The two countries also supported the permanent and peaceful settlement of the Israeli–Palestinian conflict by drawing all parties of the dispute, including Hamas, to the bargaining table.

The civil war in Syria, however, became a major breaking point between Turkey and Russia as the two countries found themselves in opposite camps regarding the conflict. While the Turkish government lent its political, economic and military support to the opposition groups that aimed to bring about the removal of the current regime, Russia stood firmly by al-Assad and shielded his administration in the UN Security Council against sanctions.

This chapter will look into the major points of convergence and divergence between Turkey and Russia regarding the changed political atmosphere and conditions in Tunisia, Egypt, Libya and Syria in the wake of the internal rebellions in these states against the oppressive and corrupt management of the long-standing rulers.

The Arab awakening and its impact on Turkish–Russian relations in the Middle East

The Arab world from North Africa to Middle East was shaken by massive waves of protests, riots and calls for bringing down of the perennial restrictive regimes starting from the end of 2010 to early 2012. The civil and military uprisings precipitated the downfall of the long-standing imperious rulers in Tunisia, Egypt, Libya and Yemen. The government in Bahrain could quash the rebellion by inviting foreign army units from Saudi Arabia and other Gulf Cooperation Council countries to the country. The most violent and intractable insurrection took place in Syria which has been engulfed in a fierce civil war for more than five years that has caused the loss of hundreds of thousands of lives.

Tunisia and Egypt

The seeds of this large-scale upheaval were planted in Tunisia in December 2010 when a street vendor immolated himself following the confiscation of his wares by the municipality and the ill-treatment he was subjected to at the hands of the local officials. This incident sparked off widespread demonstrations organized by angry crowds who were unhappy with the political, economic and social situation in the country. The intense protests brought an end to the administration of the President Zine El Abidine Ben Ali on January 14, 2011 after more than 20 years in office.

Neither Russia nor Turkey had close political and economic relations with the Ben Ali regime so it did not take long for both of them to embrace the new government. Russian President Medvedev in his address at the World Economic Forum in Davos on January 26, 2011 emphasized that what had happened in Tunisia was a big lesson for governments all around the world. He stated that when governments failed to keep with social change and failed to meet people's hopes, disorganization and chaos ensued. Medvedev also added that the governments must still remain in dialogue with all the different groups in the society in order not to lose their real foundation even if they found many of the demands made unacceptable (President of Russia 2011a). Moscow also gave its backing to the new government in Tunisia later on. In his March 2014 visit to Tunisia, Russian Foreign Minister Lavrov repeated his country's support for the political transition in the country through investment and tourism ("Russia Supports" 2014).

Turkish Minister of Foreign Affairs Ahmet Davutoğlu became one of the first top foreign officials to visit Tunisia after the change of government in February 2011. Davutoğlu remarked that Turkey declared its support for the Tunisian revolution from day one, considering that the demands and expressions of Tunisian people were right (Özhan, Davutoğlu, and Abdessalem 2012, 7). Subsequent reciprocal high-level visits at presidential, prime ministerial and ministerial levels followed. The two countries signed the Treaty of Friendship and Cooperation during Turkish Premier Erdoğan's visit to Tunisia in September 2011 which called for organization of annual meetings at the premier level. Turkey also granted 500 million dollars credit to the Tunisian businessmen through Turkish Eximbank and opened a TİKA office to support local development projects and provide assistance in , agricultural development, irrigation, energy, education and fighting disease (Algan 2012, 76–7).

The revolutionary fervor spread to Egypt at the end of January 2011 and resulted in the overthrow of the 30-year reign of President Hosni Mubarak on February 11, 2011. The candidate of the Muslim Brotherhood Mohamed Morsi won the presidential elections that took place in May–June 2012 and became the first democratically elected Head of State in Egypt.

Egypt had been a key ally of the Soviet Union for nearly two decades during the presidency of Gamal Abdel Nasser. Moscow lent its political, economic and military support to Cairo generously during this time; 97 industrial facilities were built in Egypt with Soviet aid, many of which still continue to play a significant role in Egypt's economy. The Soviet Union also sent more than 11,000 military advisers to Egypt between the years 1955 and 1976, in addition to military supplies amounting to nine billion dollars (Kreutz 2007, 111–5). These cordial relations, however, soured to a great extent when Nasser's successor Anwar Sadat decided to make a radical U-turn in his country's foreign policy line by hammering out a separate peace deal with Israel and drawing close to the USA. This new situation culminated in the unilateral abrogation of the Soviet–Egyptian Treaty of Friendship by Egypt in March 1976 and the expulsion of Soviet military officers and technicians from the country (Kreutz 2007, 115).

The bilateral relations entered into a steady trend in the post-Cold War era during the presidency of the Mubarak although they never entertained the high level enjoyed during the heydays of the Cold War.

The bilateral trade between the two countries remained in meager proportions. In 2010 it amounted to 2.1 billion dollars, Egypt becoming thirty-fourth largest trade partner of Russia (Issaev 2011). The country, on the other hand, became the second most popular destination after Turkey for the Russian tourists. In 2009, 17 percent of the Russian tourists going abroad for their vacations stopped by Egypt (Issaev 2011).

In line with the low degree of primacy of Egypt in Russian foreign policy, Moscow's reaction to the fall of Mubarak had been low-profile and cautious. Underlining the importance of restoration of the democratic processes in Egypt, Russian President Medvedev recalled the long-standing multifaceted ties between his country and Egypt and expressed his desire to develop them further in the new period (President of Russia 2011b). Russian Foreign Minister Lavrov paid a visit to Egypt in March 2011 and Egyptian Minister of Foreign Affairs Mohamed Kamel Amr reciprocated this visit in December 2011. Following the meeting, the two sides highlighted the importance of renewal from July 2011 of Russian supplies of grain to Egypt and further development of touristic relations (Ministry of Foreign Affairs of the Russian Federation 2011).

The Muslim Brotherhood had been on Russia's list of terrorist organizations since 2003 owing to its activities in the North Caucasus during the Chechen War (Trenin 2013, 15). Moscow, however, decided to take the pragmatic line by focusing its economic interests in Egypt and the Russian President Putin received his counterpart Morsi in Kremlin in April 2013 (President of Russia 2013a). Yet, Russia obviously did not shed any tears when Morsi was toppled after a military coup in July 2013 as the leader of the coup, First Deputy Prime Minister, Minister of Defense and Military Industry Abdel Fattah al-Sisi was welcomed warmly by Putin in February 2014. While the two sides stressed the development of economic and people-to-people ties between the two countries (President of Russia 2013b), there were also rumors that al-Sisi inked deals to acquire Russian Rostvertol Mi-35 attack helicopters and Mi-17 multi-purpose helicopters (Schenker and Trager 2014).

Different from Russia which adopted a pragmatic and flexible foreign policy stand with respect to Egypt that focused on its material gains, Turkey deviated from its traditional cautious and conservative wait-and-see approach when the demonstrations against the rule of Mubarak commenced in Egypt and gave its full backing to the protestors. Turkish Premier Erdoğan was the first leader in Europe and the Middle East who called on Mubarak to heed the people's outcry and meet their demands for change ("Turkish PM Erdoğan" 2011). Moreover, Turkish President Gül became the first head of state to visit Egypt in March 2011 in the aftermath of the ousting of Mubarak (Republic of Turkey Ministry of Foreign Affairs 2011).

The election of Morsi to the Presidency of Egypt was hailed instantly and wholeheartedly by the AKP government which advised the Muslim Brotherhood to follow Turkey's lead by forming a transparent and democratic political order without ignoring the principle of secularism. The cadres of the Muslim Brotherhood and the AKP had come from similar Islamist roots and the two groups had enjoyed close bonds in the past. AKP considered that, similar to its own experience, the election victory of the Muslim Brotherhood in Egypt would give the movement the political legitimacy it had been seeking for years. Egypt under the rule of Brotherhood might also become more eager to countenance the AKP policies regarding the Middle Eastern affairs, especially the Palestinian-Israeli conflict.

The events in Egypt, however, did not unfold in the direction Turkey predicted. Probably emanating from its over-engagement with the Brotherhood, Ankara could not foresee the growing discomfort and dissatisfaction brewing against the Morsi administration among the other segments of the Egyptian society. Much to the chagrin and surprise of Ankara, Morsi fell from grace in a military coup after barely more than one year in office. Turkey denounced the coup immediately and vehemently and diplomatic relations between the two countries were downgraded to the level of *chargé d'affaires*. Relations between Ankara and Cairo are currently at the lowest ebb, similar to the early 1950s. Turkey's ideological and rigid policy that did not leave much room for political maneuvering put it in an extremely difficult position in Egypt. Furthermore, it jeopardized the interests of the Turkish business community in the country which realized investments worth two billion dollars.

Libya

A few days after Mubarak resigned, an armed rebellion against the 42-year administration of Muammar Gaddafi commenced in Libya. Different from the Tunisian and Egyptian cases, substantial parts of the army took the side of the regime in Libya and drove back the attacks of the opposition forces with success. Gaddafi fell in August 2011 only after a bombing campaign spearheaded by France, the United Kingdom and the USA buttressed by the establishment of a no-fly zone over Libya, through a UN mandate tipped the balance in favor of the rebel forces.

Both Turkey and Russia had been awarded with lucrative trade contracts with the Gaddafi regime and realized significant investments in the country. In return for the cancellation of its four-and-a-half billion Soviet-era debt in April 2008, the Libyan government had signed eight billion-dollar deals with the Russian firms which opened the energy, defense and construction sectors of the country to their business ventures (Malashenko 2013, 12). Turkey had more than ten billion dollars of investment in Libya, especially in the construction sector. Libya was the most important market for Turkish contractors in Africa as proven by the presence of more than 25,000 Turkish workers in the country (Sümer 2013, 20). These extensive economic ties prevented both Turkey and Russia at the initial phase of the clashes from choosing a side to support. Turkish Prime Minister Erdoğan even stated that NATO's intervention in Libya was out of the question and Turkey was against it ("Erdogan Rules Out" 2011).

It did not take much, however, for Moscow and Ankara to change course regarding foreign military intervention in NATO. Both of the states realized before long that the intervention would occur with or without their approval, therefore they decided on a bandwagoning strategy in order not to be unseated from the table where the states in favor of a military attack would sit and share the spoils in a post-Gaddafi environment. Russia supported the UN Security Council Resolution 1970 on February 26, 2011 which stipulated an embargo on arms exports to Libya and abstained from voting of the UN Security Council Resolution 1973 on March 17, 2011, which anticipated the formation of a no-fly zone over Libyan airspace. Turkey, on the other hand, did not send any troops to Libya under NATO command to fight against pro-Gaddafi military units, but did not hesitate to dispatch a naval force to the country on March 25, 2011 to enforce the blockade of ports under regime's control (Tuğal 2012, 14).

Turkey quickly adapted to the post-Gaddafi era in Libya. Ankara extended a 200-million dollars aid package to the Libyan opposition (Gümüşçü 2012). Foreign Minister Davutoğlu went to Libya one day after the opposition forces captured Tripoli. Turkish Premier Erdoğan was the first foreign leader to visit the country after the overthrow of Gaddafi. Bilateral trade, as well as Turkish investments in construction, manufacturing and agricultural sectors increased (Republic of Turkey Ministry of Economy 2013) as a result of the good rapport between Ankara and the new government in Tripoli.

The Libyan experience was a complete disappointment for Russia. Although the new Libyan government renewed the contracts of the Western companies dated from the Gaddafi period, it did not honor the Russian deals (Trenin 2013, 6–7). Moreover, Russia felt quite uncomfortable with the outcome of the UN mandate in Libya as an intervention which aimed to protect civilians against the atrocities of the regime in the first place ended up striving for and eventually accomplishing regime change (Lavrov 2011). This feeling of being sidelined became decisive pertaining to the formulation of Russian policy in Syria and urged Russia to be more careful and scrupulous with respect to resolutions concluded in the Security Council in the ensuing days.

Syria

The most bloody and protracted chapter of the Arab insurrection has been going on in Syria since the spring of 2011 which has taken an increasingly religious and sectarian character that has claimed the lives of hundreds of thousands of Syrian citizens and brought regional and global powers into the conflict in one way or another. The civil war in Syria brought forth an explicit disagreement and difference of policy between Turkey and Russia regarding the future of the regime in Damascus. While Turkey is openly and vigorously seeking to bring down the administration of al-Assad, Russia continues to stand strongly by al-Assad and has extended its support to the current regime on many platforms, most crucially in the UN Security Council.

Russia's deep and multifaceted ties with Syria date back to Cold War years. Damascus had been the most enduring and loyal ally of Moscow at that time. Although Russia had lost its interest and ardor pertaining to Middle Eastern matters for a while in the early years of the post-Cold War period, it nevertheless attached special importance to the preservation of political and military ties with Syria. The two sides signed a military-technical cooperation agreement in April 1994 which resumed the sales of Russian arms and military hardware to Syria (Kreutz 2007, 20). Between 1991 and 2012, Russia alone provided 44 percent of Syria's military arsenal ("Syrian Arms Imports" 2013, 8). It also continued to send military advisers to Syria, accepted Syrian students to Russian universities and sent off Russian officers to lecture at Syria's military officer training academy. Russia retains a sophisticated listening facility in Latakia which is quite useful for collecting intelligence regarding the region in addition to the naval resupply site in Tartus.

Damascus and Moscow carried on good relations in the post-Cold War era on the political front as well. The two countries circumvented each other's thorny issues. Syria regarded the Chechen conflict as an internal problem for Russia and refrained from criticizing Moscow on international platforms. Moreover, Syria was one of the few countries that had explicitly supported Russian actions and standing concerning the situation in South Ossetia (President of Russia 2008). In return Russia backed up Syria in its call to Israel for the return of Golan Heights to its sovereignty and opposed the imposition of military sanctions on the Syrian regime based on alleged involvement of some Syrian officials in the murder of former Lebanese Prime Minister Rafiq al-Hariri.

A change of leadership in Syria would mean for Russia not only the loss of a reliable ally that had proved its fealty in tough times and under difficult conditions but also its possible replacement with an Islamist government which might act inimically to Russian national interests. Russia was worried and uncomfortable that the impact and outreach of radical Islamist factions in the Syrian opposition backed by Saudi and Qatari funds might spread to Russian territory and incite disturbance among its Muslim population which might again fan separatist currents in the Northern Caucasus, especially in Chechnya, as it had done in the past. The head of the Russian Security Service Alexander Bortnikov's statement that it would be very likely that the extremist forces located in Syria would soon begin to infiltrate the Muslim regions of southern Russia and destabilize the situation in the traditionally problematic republics of Dagestan, Ingushetia and Chechnya (Kozhanov 2013, 29) demonstrated clearly the gravity of this Russian apprehension concerning the ascendance and prevalence of radical Islamist movements in Russia's neighborhood. Russia was more annoyed with Saudi Arabia which had allocated considerable manpower and generous funds to the Chechen cause in the past and felt that a similar scenario was taking place in Syria where an all-out war was waged against a secular government with all the political, economic and military means possible. The Syrian conflict tensed up Saudi-Russian relations as well by spoiling the rapprochement process commenced between the two countries in the early 2000s via cooperation attempts in the economic sphere. While the Saudi Foreign Minister Prince Saud Al-Faisal accused Russia of contributing to the 'genocide' perpetrated by the Syrian government through provision of arms (Al-Thumali and Al-Ghabiri 2013), Russian Foreign Ministry Representative on Human Rights, Democracy and the Rule of Law Konstantin Dolgov criticized the Saudi administration for its heavy-handed suppression of a protest in the Eastern Province where the majority of the people were of Shia faith and major oil reserves along with industrial facilities were concentrated ("Saudi Arabia Surprised with" 2012).

Turkey and Syria were hardly on friendly terms during the Cold War years because the two states had been members of rival power blocs. Ankara and Damascus continued to be distant neighbors in the post-Cold War era due to the existence of myriad bilateral issues in the relationship ranging from Syria's claim over Hatay which was located within the boundaries of Turkey, a dispute over water, Syria's support to PKK by hosting its leader Öcalan in the country plus lending logistical, military and financial assistance to the separatist organization and Turkey's signing defense agreements with Israel. Turkish–Syrian relations entered a remarkable process of reconciliation after Syria's expulsion of Öcalan from the country in October 1998, the closure of PKK training camps on the Syrian land and the cuting-off of logistical support for the organization (Altunışık and Tür 2006, 238). The likelihood of the dismemberment of Iraq on ethnic and confessional lines after the US occupation of the country, in contrast to the continuous strivings of both of the states' in opposite direction and Syria's deliberate decision to draw near to Turkey to break out of its isolation on the international stage which intensified after the Syrian administration was accused of devising and soliciting the murder of Lebanon's former prime minister, al-Hariri, in February 2005, brought the two neighbors closer and converged their policies on the region.

Syria had to face its own Kurdish problem in March 2004 when clashes broke out between its Arab and Kurdish populations following the incidents between these two groups at a football match in Qamishli, in northern part of the country close to the Iraq border (Kazancı 2004, 10). The Qamishli event sparked off a firmer stance in Syria in dealing with the Kurdish separatism and motivated it further toward cooperating with Turkey in containment of the PKK. Syria arrested local PKK members and handed them over to the Turkish security personnel; Ankara and Damascus also founded consultation mechanisms to exchange views on regional matters and to cope effectively with crime and terrorism (Bar 2006, 47–8). Moreover, on April 26–9, 2009, for the first time in their history, the land forces of Turkey and Syria performed joint military exercises to increase training and operational capabilities of the respective border units and to deal more efficaciously with smugglers and the PKK militants operating along the border ("Turkey and Syria" 2009).

Turkey served as a conduit to Syria in its engagement with the outside world especially after the country was blacklisted by the US government owing to its support for the resistance movement in Iraq, its alleged role in the assassination of al-Hariri and the covert activities of the Syrian intelligence organization, Al-Muhaberat in Lebanon (Vurmay 2005, 8). Turkey advocated Syria in its attempt to reach a rapprochement with Israel and the two states started indirect peace talks under the auspices of Turkey (Republic of Turkey Ministry of Foreign Affairs 2008). After four rounds of negotiations, the peace process was discontinued because of Israel's offensive on Gaza Strip in December 2008.

Along with the mounting political and security ties, the two states also developed the commercial facet of their relationship. Notable moves in this direction were the signature of the Free Trade Agreement between Turkey and Syria during Turkish Prime Minister Erdoğan's visit to the country on December 22–23, 2004 (Hale 2007, 136), the foundation of the Syrian–Turkish High-Level Strategic Cooperation Council on September 16, 2009 (Sabbagh 2009) and the abolition of visa requirements between the two states on October 13, 2009 ("Turkey and Syria" 2009). Furthermore, Turkey and Syria, along with Jordan and Lebanon, declared the establishment of Quadripartite High-Level Cooperation Council on June 10, 2010 to create a zone of free movement of goods and persons among themselves (Republic of Turkey Ministry of Foreign Affairs 2010). Syria also became an important transit country for Turkey for the delivery of Turkish goods to other states in the Middle East.

This elevating and promising relationship received a heavy blow in the summer of 2011, when the al-Assad regime in fear of losing its power and control in the country in face of massive protests against its administration inspired by the similar rallies in Tunisia, Egypt and Libya decided to quell the uprising with tough military measures. After its pressure and suggestions on al-Assad for constitutional reform and reaching a compromise with the protestors, especially with the political wing of the Syrian Muslim Brotherhood fell on deaf ears, the AKP government made a radical break in its foreign policy and opted fervently for a regime change in Damascus. Ankara bestowed its political support to the Syrian National Council, provided arms, logistical support and training facilities to the Free Syrian Army and welcomed nearly 1 million Syrian refugees fleeing from the country in the midst of military clashes between the government forces and the opposition units. However, the escalation of the military conflict into a civil war in which regional countries such as Iraq and Iran and non-state actors like Hezbollah intervened on the side of the Baath administration along with global players such as China and Russia that extended support to the regime through vetoing of sanctions at the UN Security Council, the continuous increase in the number of the Syrian refugees seeking shelter in Turkey, coupled with growing unease among the local population in the cities where these people lived, the economic losses Turkey faced due to cutting off trade with Syria and finally the Western world's reluctance to carry out a military operation to contribute to the removal of al-Assad from power undermined Turkey's Syrian policy to a great extent and revealed its weaknesses and limitations.

Turkey was aware of the fact that the al-Assad regime would not survive for long without the diplomatic, military and financial support of Russia. Four times Russia, along with China, vetoed resolutions that threatened sanctions against the Syrian government in the UN Security Council. Russia provided weapons and military equipment to the Syrian army and took Syria's crude oil in exchange for refined oil products (Borshchevskaya 2013). Furthermore, Moscow lent Syria loans and credit to hinder possible financial bankruptcy.

Relying on its strong economic and promising political ties with Russia, Turkey in the early phase of the Syrian conflict carried out many telephone conversations with the Russian leadership and made visits to Russia to persuade them to drop their unequivocal backing of the Syrian regime. However, after Russia resorted to its veto power in the UN Security Council to block resolutions against the al-Assad administration, Turkey, although in vague wording, accused Russia of acting irresponsibly (Republic of Turkey Ministry of Foreign Affairs 2012).

The outbreak of an unpleasant incident in October 2012 portended the emergence of strained relations between Turkey and Russia pertaining to Syria. On October 10, Turkey forced a Syrian passenger plane en route from Moscow to Damascus to land and declared that it had impounded the Russian munitions on board intended for the Syrian government (Kardaş 2012, 1). However the forced landing of the Russian plane by Turkish officials did not stop President Putin from visiting Turkey in December 2012 to attend the High-Level Russian-Turkish Cooperation Council. The two sides signed 11 agreements in the fields of energy, credit and finance, and culture. In the press meeting following the consultations, Putin conceded frankly that they could not find a common position in terms of the methods they applied for the settlement of the Syrian conflict (President of Russia 2012). He also added that despite not being the absolute supporter of the Syrian regime, Russia had concerns with respect to the post-Assad Syria by drawing parallels to the situation in Libya succeeding the removal of Gaddafi, especially the killing of American ambassador in Benghazi by radical Islamist groups.

Russia's commencement of airstrikes starting from September 30, 2015 at the behest of al-Assad became another watershed in the Turkish–Russian association. Although Putin declared that Russia's military operation in Syria aimed to support the regime in its fight against terrorist groups (President of Russia 2015), Russia's bombing of some anti-government Islamic groups close to Turkey, especially the Turkmen inhabitants of the Jabal Turkmen region in northern Latakia, elicited a significant rupture in relations which started with a few words of reproach and culminated in Turkey's downing of the Russian Sukhoi Su-24M bomber in November 2015.

The gradual normalization of Turkish–Russian relations following Erdoğan's letter to Putin necessitates re-examination and revision of Turkey's Syrian policy which might open more room for joint work towards resolution of the Syrian impasse. Cooperation and policy coordination between Ankara and Moscow is quite important to ensure cessation of hostilities between the warring parties, provision of humanitarian aid to Syrian people and attainment of a workable political solution in Syria.

The Middle East has been added to the agenda of post-Cold War Turkish–Russian relationship as a new and knotty item in the recent years. The discussions revolved around the nuclear program of Iran, and the civil war in Syria drew attention of both Ankara and Moscow to this volatile and conflict-ridden region. The Russian and Turkish policies pertaining to the civil war in Syria were diametrically opposed, as each granted its obvious and intense support to the different parties of the conflict which resulted in an open confrontation between them that nearly derailed the promising rapport which had been threaded carefully and delicately in the last decade with the great efforts of officials, businessmen, intellectuals and ordinary citizens.

The increasing weight and impact of Turkish and Russian presidents on foreign policy decision-making processes had a considerable part in prolonging the November 2015 crisis as well. Both Erdoğan and Putin were anxious about the possible loss of support that might occur in the event of backing down after initiating and escalating a crisis. However, a rally round-the-flag effect was short-term, especially for Turkey as the breakdown of multidimensional ties with Russia had damaging results for well-being of the political supporters of Erdoğan who urged him to look for ways to rekindle the frozen relationship. So although expanding political, economic and social-cultural ties did not suffice to prevent appealing to military force in the Syrian case, contrary to the assumptions of the complex interdependency theory, the use of force by Turkey had costly effects on the non-security goals of the country as the theory anticipated (Keohane and Nye 1977, 29) and led Ankara to change its policy.

Both Turkey and Russia have various significant interests at stake in a wide area ranging from the Balkans to the Middle East, encompassing the Black Sea, the South Caucasus and the Central Asia regions. This vast area abounds with frozen conflicts, dormant flashpoints along with active armed clashes. The detailed and in-depth examination in this part has demonstrated that except for the Black Sea, the views, policies as well as acts of Ankara and Moscow differed noticeably from each other with regard to the many issue areas in these regions in the past two decades.

The absence of common institutions in the South Caucasus and Middle East, that might act as platforms for deliberation, negotiation and even harmonization of disputed foreign policy matters, left the development of the relationship to the whim of strong leaders which floundered to a great extent in times of discord, as had been the case in the plane incident of November 2015. The establishment of joint organizations in areas of common interests which will also embrace the other regional states might act as safety valves against possible future crises by providing an opportunity for discussion of possible areas of disagreement and implementation of emergency measures when needed.

The final part of the book will throw light on the most advanced and vibrant aspect of the Turkish–Russian relationship, the growing and diversifying economic bonds between the two countries, which have been the major driving force of post-Cold War Turkish–Russian rapprochement by examining bilateral cooperation in the fields of trade, energy, construction and investment.

References

Al-Thumali, Fayez, and Asma Al-Ghabiri. 2013. "Saudi Foreign Minister Says Syrians Facing Genocide." *Asharq Al-Awsat*, June 26.

Algan, Akın. 2012. "The 'January 14 Revolution' in Tunisia and Turkish-Tunisian Relations." *Turkish Policy Quarterly* 10(4): 73–78.

Altunışık, Meliha Benli, and Özlem Tür. 2006. "From Distant Neighbors to Partners? Changing Syrian-Turkish Relations." *Security Dialogue* 37(2): 229–248.

Bar, Allon. 2006. "Turkish Foreign Policy Survey: Directions and Dilemmas in 2007." *Perceptions (Journal of International Affairs)* 11(3): 37–57.
Borshchevskaya, Anna. 2013. "Russia's Many Interests in Syria." *The Washington Institute*, January 24.
Dünya, "Erdogan Rules Out Possibility of NATO Intervention in Libya." 2011. March 2.
Gümüşçü, Şebnem. 2012. "Turkey's Reactions to the Arab Spring." *Yale Journal of International Affairs*, May 16.
Hale, William. 2007. *Turkey, the US and Iraq.* London: SAQI.
Hürriyet, "Turkish PM Erdoğan Urges Mubarak to Heed Egyptian Outcry." 2011. February 1.
Issaev, Leonid. 2011. "Russia Says Goodbye to Egypt." *Russian International Affairs Council*, September 10.
Kardaş, Şaban. 2012. "Sailing in Uncharted Waters: Turkish and Russian Divergence in Syria." *GMF*: 1–4. Accessed November 1, 2016. http://www.gmfus.org/publications/sailing-uncharted-waters-turkish-and-russian-divergence-syria/.
Kazancı, Hicran. 2004. "Suriye'nin Elinde Patlayan 'Kürt Kozu'." *Strateji* 1 (7): 10.
Keohane, Robert O., and Joseph S. Nye Jr. 1977. *Power and Interdependence: World Politics in Transition.* Boston: Little Brown.
Kozhanov, Nikolay. 2013. "Russian Support for Assad's Regime: Is There a Red Line?" *The International Spectator: Italian Journal of International Affairs* 48(2): 25–31.
Kreutz, Andrej. 2007. *Russia in the Middle East: Friend or Foe?* Westport: Praeger Security International.
Lavrov, Sergey. 2011. "International Relations in a Turbulence Zone: Where are the Points of Support?" *Ministry of Foreign Affairs of the Russian Federation.* Accessed April 12, 2014. http://www.mid.ru/bdomp/BRP_4.nsf/f68cd37b84711611c3256f6d00541094/d126fa2fc8ff917b4425798200209721!/.
Malashenko, Alexey. 2013. *Russia and the Arab Spring.* Moscow: Carnegie Moscow Center.
Ministry of Foreign Affairs of the Russian Federation. 2011. "Talks between Russian Foreign Minister Sergey Lavrov and Egyptian Foreign Minister Mohamed Kamel Amr." *Ministry of Foreign Affairs of the Russian Federation.* Accessed April 6, 2014. http://www.mid.ru/bdomp/brp_4.nsf/e78a48070f128a7b43256999005bcbb3/0eb95039746c795d442579750033c11d!/.
Özhan, Taha, Ahmet Davutoğlu, and Rafik Abdessalem. 2012. "Arab Spring, Tunisia and Turkey." *SETA*, no. 7: 1–16.
President of Russia. 2008. "Dmitry Medvedev Met with President of Syria Bashar al-Assad." *President of Russia.* Accessed April 19, 2014. http://www.kremlin.ru/eng/text/themes/2008/08/211308_205584.shtml/.
President of Russia. 2011a. "Dmitry Medvedev Addressed the World Economic Forum in Davos." *President of Russia.* Accessed April 6, 2014. http://eng.kremlin.ru/news/1684/.

President of Russia. 2011b. "Statement by the President of Russia on the Situation in Egypt." *President of Russia*. Accessed April 6, 2014. http://eng.kremlin.ru/news/1768/.

President of Russia. 2012. "Working Visit to Turkey." *President of Russia*. Accessed April 20, 2014. http://eng.kremlin.ru/news/4690/.

President of Russia. 2013a. "Press Statements Following Russian-Egyptian Talks." *President of Russia*. Accessed April 6, 2014. http://eng.kremlin.ru/transcripts/5305/.

President of Russia. 2013b. "Meeting with Defense and Foreign Ministers of Egypt." *President of Russia*. Accessed April 6, 2014. http://eng.kremlin.ru/news/6656.

President of Russia. 2015. "Meeting with Government Members." *President of Russia*. Accessed July 27, 2016. http://en.kremlin.ru/events/president/news/50401/.

Republic of Turkey Ministry of Economy. 2013. "Countries & Regions-Africa-Libya." *Republic of Turkey Ministry of Economy*. Accessed April 12, 2014. http://www.economy.gov.tr/index.cfm?sayfa=countriesandregions&country=LY&region=0/.

Republic of Turkey Ministry of Foreign Affairs. 2008. "Press Release Regarding the Indirect Peace Talks between Syria and Israel under the Auspices of Turkey." *Republic of Turkey Ministry of Foreign Affairs*. Accessed April 19, 2014. http://www.mfa.gov.tr/no-81—21-may-2008_-press-release-regarding-the-indirect-peace-talks-between-syria-and-israel-under-the-auspices-of-turkey-_unofficial-translation_.en.mfa/.

Republic of Turkey Ministry of Foreign Affairs. 2010. "Joint Political Declaration on the Establishment of the High Level Cooperation Council among Turkey, Syria, Jordan and Lebanon." *Republic of Turkey Ministry of Foreign Affairs*. Accessed April 19, 2014. http://www.mfa.gov.tr/joint-political-declaration-on-the-esthablishement-of-the-high-level-cooperation-council-among-turkey_-syria_-jordan-and-lebanon.en.mfa/.

Republic of Turkey Ministry of Foreign Affairs. 2011. "Relations between Turkey-Egypt." *Republic of Turkey Ministry of Foreign Affairs*. Accessed April 6, 2014. http://www.mfa.gov.tr/relations-between-turkey-egypt.en.mfa/.

Republic of Turkey Ministry of Foreign Affairs. 2012. "Press Release Regarding the UN Security Council Being Unable to Reach a Decision on Syria." *Republic of Turkey Ministry of Foreign Affairs*. Accessed April 20, 2014. http://www.mfa.gov.tr/no_-38_-4-february-2012_-press-release-regarding-the-un-security-council-being-unable-to-reach-a-decision-on-syria.en.mfa/.

Russian Analytical Digest, "Syrian Arms Imports 1991–2012 by Country of Origin (in US Dollars, Constant 1990 Prices)." 2013, no. *Russian Analytical Digest* 128: 1–12.

Sabbagh, H. 2009. "First Ministerial Meeting of the Syrian-Turkish Strategic Cooperation Council Concluded, Long-Term Strategic Partnership between the Two Countries Established." *SANA*, October 14.

Schenker, David, and Eric Trager. 2014. "Egypt's Arms Deal with Russia: Potential Strategic Costs." *Washington Institute Policy Watch*, March 4.

Sümer, Fahrettin. 2013. "Turkey's Changing Foreign Policy and the Arab Spring." *The Innovation Journal: The Public Sector Innovation Journal* 18 (1): 1–28.

TASS, "Saudi Arabia Surprised with Statement by Dolgov on Eastern Province." 2012. July 15.

The Anatolia News Agency, "Turkey and Syria to Stage Joint Military Exercise." 2009. April 26.

Trenin, Dmitri. 2013. *The Mythical Alliance: Russia's Syria Policy*. Moscow: The Carnegie Papers.

TRT World, "Turkey and Syria Abolish Visa Requirements." 2009. October 14.

Tuğal, Cihan. 2012. "Democratic Janissaries: Turkey's Role in the Arab Spring." *New Left Review* 76: 5–24.

Vurmay, H. Miray. 2005. "Değisen Dengeler, Gelisen İlişkiler Doğrultusunda Türkiye-Suriye İlişkileri." *Strateji* 1(52): 7–8.

Xinhua, "Russia Supports Tunisia's Political Transition: Lavrov." 2014. March 3.

Part III
Consolidation of economic association

7 Broadening and deepening of economic bonds

The second premise of complex interdependency theory points at the expanding and diversifying state of foreign policy agendas' of the countries and underlines that military security is no longer the preponderant item on the agenda (Keohane and Nye 1977, 26). Human rights issues, identity matters, environmental problems, infectious diseases, immigration and poverty all took their place on the list as compelling and challenging subjects. The post-Cold War world especially witnessed the growing significance of economic security for the survival of states. Coping with inflation and unemployment, achieving stable economic growth, raising the living standards of the population and ensuring the welfare of citizens spurred the politicians to take into consideration the economic matters even in foreign policy-making to accomplish electoral success. So, economic bonds between countries have become as equally important as the political and military ties for the foundation of a healthy and sustainable relationship. This situation found its manifest reflection in post-Cold War Turkish–Russian relations as well.

The growing and expanding Turkish–Russian relationship owed much of its success to the strengthening and diversifying of economic ties between the two countries in the immediate post-Cold War period. Despite being at loggerheads with each other regarding political issues during the better part of the 1990s, Turkey and Russia steadily and continuously managed to develop the economic and commercial aspect of their association in those years. Two important mechanisms that were established in the post-Cold War era contributed to a great extent to the consolidation and institutionalization of the economic links between the two countries. The first one was the Turkish–Russian Joint Economic Commission which was founded on May 14, 1992 in accordance with the Trade and Economic Cooperation Agreement concluded between the parties (State Planning Organization 1992). The main aim of the Commission was to revise the existing commercial-economic relations between the two states, take action to smooth out the points of disagreement and galvanize efforts to advance economic relations to a level which satisfied the interests of both of the parties. It usually worked as a preparatory organ which set the stage for the economic agreements and protocols that would be signed between the two countries.

The second mechanism was the Turkish–Russian Business Council formed in 1991 as part of the Foreign Economic Relations Board (DEİK) of Turkey. DEİK was constituted in 1988 to pave the way for Turkey's economic, commercial, industrial and financial relations with foreign countries as well as international business communities (DEİK 2013). It acted as an intermediary between the public and private sectors by bringing together state officials and representatives of the business community. The Turkish–Russian Business Council which operated under the umbrella of DEİK was composed of companies that already had business relations or planned to develop such relations in each country. The Council organized joint gatherings, exhibitions, fairs, conferences, seminars, symposiums and information meetings to inform Turkish and Russian businessmen of existing business opportunities in Turkey and Russia and to acquaint them with the economic outlook, business environment and legislation in each country.

The promising economic relations of the immediate post-Cold War period continued in a rising trend in the succeeding years despite short-term disruptions triggered by the upheavals in the economies of Russia and Turkey precipitated by the financial crises of 1998 and 2001 and global recession of 2008. Energy cooperation rose to higher levels with the completion of the Blue Stream pipeline project that transported Russian natural gas directly to Turkey, and Russia's construction of Turkey's first nuclear power plant. Mutual investments grew in size and varied in scope. Not only small and medium-sized firms but also big Turkish conglomerates as well as prominent Russian state and private corporations carried out investments in each other's country. This chapter will examine the expanding and thriving economic relations between Turkey and Russia which played a determining and fundamental role on the advance of political relations between the two countries by focusing on trade, energy, construction and contracting services and investment areas which witnessed the utmost cooperation between the two states throughout the years.

Bilateral trade

Bilateral trade between Turkey and Russia which was worth about one and a half billion dollars in 1992 in the wake of the Cold War rose to more than 31 billion dollars in 2014 (Turkish Institute of Statistics 2015), making Russia Turkey's second biggest trade partner after Germany. The 3.7 percent contraction in the Russian economy triggered by the decline in oil prices along with the Western sanctions over Russia's annexation of Crimea brought about a 10 percent decrease in retail sales in Russia (Amos 2016) which negatively affected Turkish–Russian commerce.

Turkish–Russian trade dropped to 24 billion dollars in 2015, Russia becoming Turkey's third largest trade partner after Germany and China (Turkish Institute of Statistics 2016a). Russia ranked eleventh in Turkey's exports and third in its imports whereas Turkey held the twelfth place in Russia's import figures (ITC Trade Map 2016a) and ninth place in Russia's export statistics (ITC Trade Map 2016b). Turkey's trade with Russia formed nearly 7 percent of its total trade, whereas Russia's trade with Turkey made up of nearly 5 percent of its total trade in 2015. Russia's ban on some of Turkish goods in the wake of the plane incident of November 2015 impaired the bilateral trade relations to a considerable extent in 2016 as demonstrated by the second-quarter trade records. While bilateral trade between Turkey and Russia came at nearly 13 billion dollars between January and June 2015, it dwindled to 8.5 billion dollars one year later, registering nearly a 60 percent decrease in Turkey's exports to Russia (Turkish Institute of Statistics 2016b). Russia's lifting of sanctions on Turkey following the thaw in June 2016, although it seemed to take place in a slow and gradual manner, might restore former close commercial bonds between the two countries.

The complementary character of the Turkish and Russian economies led to a considerable boom in commerce between the two countries in the post-Cold War period. Turkey sells textile products, fruit, vegetables, electrical machines and motorized vehicles to Russia and in return buys fossil fuels, metals, coal, fertilizer, grain and chemicals. The trade imbalance between the two countries has been growing exponentially throughout the years to the disadvantage of Turkey. In 2015 while Turkish exports to Russia came at about 3.6 billion dollars, Turkish imports from Russia exceeded 20 billion dollars (Turkish Institute of Statistics 2016a).

One should look into the details of the traded items between Turkey and Russia in order to understand the reasons of this trade disparity.

Textile merchandise and the consumer goods which Turkey sent to Russia were mostly replaced with their domestic equivalents during times of financial crisis. The goods Turkey imported from Russia, on the other hand, could not be replaced easily as they were composed of energy items, metals and industrial products which Turkey was either deprived of or unable to manufacture in the domestic market. Thus, even in 2001, when the country went through one of the worst economic crises of its history, Russian exports to Turkey only dropped 12 per cent.

Turkey from time to time ran into logjams in its trade with Russia. In May 2005, Russia suspended the importation of flowers, fruit, vegetables and poultry products from Turkey on the grounds that they did not meet the health standards of the Russian Federal Veterinary and Phyto-sanitary Control Service (Arslan 2005). The ban remained in effect for four months and Turkish producers lost nearly 300 million dollars (Tekerek and Arman 2008). A similar ban on some Turkish fruit and vegetables (tomatoes, aubergines, potatoes, grapes and lemons) was put into force in June 2008 by Russian authorities after the discovery of high levels of chemical fertilizer and pesticides in these agricultural products (Daly 2008a). The two countries signed a memorandum in April 2009 to reach a final solution in the dispute. According to the agreement, in the case of non-compliance of Turkish agricultural products to Russian sanitary standards, instead of an embargo on whole Turkish exporters, the Russian state would sanction only the non-compliant company ("Rusya ile Ticarette" 2009).

Russia's full inspection of Turkey-originated goods except fruit and vegetables at customs stations starting from July 16, 2008 became a major grievance in commercial relations. The strict customs regulations and increase in customs duties set forth by the Russian state for protection and promotion of domestic production caused Turkish firms to suffer financial losses and fall behind in their competition with other exporters to the Russian market (Adem Kula, Assistant Coordinator, Turkish-Eurasian Business Council, DEİK, interview with the author, January 20, 2009). A protocol was hammered out on September 18, 2008 between the Turkish Undersecretariat of Customs and the Federal Customs Service of Russia for a simplification of the customs procedures. According to the document, the firms that gave explicit information about invoice value, tariffs and chattel papers would receive preferential treatment at the Russian customs gates (Official Gazette 2008). Despite the signing of the protocol, problems endured. Russian authorities annulled the regulation requiring the full inspection of Turkish goods at customs checkpoints on August 17, 2009, with the endorsement of a memorandum on customs procedures between the Russian and Turkish customs agencies at the time of Putin's August 6, 2009 visit to Turkey which finally resolved the matter (Murat Nesimoğlu, Moscow Embassy of the Republic of Turkey Office of the Commercial Counsellor, telephone interview with the author, October 11, 2010). Putin was determined to find a solution to the matter as in 2008 with trade volume of nearly 38 billion dollars, Russia had become for the first time Turkey's number one trade partner, surpassing Germany.

Russia's prohibition of imports of fruit, vegetables, poultry, flowers and salt from Turkey from January 1, 2016 along with strict examination of Turkish goods at Russian borders became an unpleasant episode in Turkish–Russian trade relations. The rapprochement reached between the two countries in June 2016 is expected to ameliorate this lose-lose situation. While Turkey, according to first-quarter data lost 209 million dollars in 2016 due to the embargo ("Turkey Loses" 2016), food prices in Russia increased as imports from Central European, Middle Eastern, North African and Chinese markets failed to appear as serious alternatives to Turkey due to logistical costs and legal difficulties (Nacar 2016; Has 2016).

Apart from the registered commerce between the two countries, there existed suitcase trade which was an important item in Turkey's business with Russia. Russian citizens came to Turkey with big and empty suitcases, bought mostly textile, leather and household goods from small shops in İstanbul, Trabzon, Artvin and resold them back in Russia. In the early 1990s, suitcase trade most of the time exceeded the legal trade between the two countries in terms of value. However, Turkish governments turned a blind eye to this irregular activity as it was a significant source of foreign currency and generated employment in other sectors such as accommodation, transportation and travel services. For Russia suitcase trade was equally important as approximately 30 million Russian nationals were involved in the process and this economic activity not only improved the ailing financial situation of individual Russian citizens but also provided them with consumer goods they had been deprived of for a long time. At its peak point the suitcase trade between Turkey and Russia came at 8.8 billion dollars. It is still an important item in Turkey's trade with Russia. Despite the Russian government's restrictive measures for empowerment of local small and medium-sized enterprises and to boost domestic production, the figures came at 8.6 billion dollars in 2014 (Central Bank of Turkey 2016).

Energy

Turkey and Russia started their long-term energy relationship on September 18, 1984 with the signing of a natural gas agreement which would last for 25 years and required Russia to dispatch an annual 6 billion m^3 natural gas to Turkey from 1987 (BOTAŞ 1984). Ankara would pay the gas bill with cash, manufactured foods and contracting services. This agreement not only initiated long-standing energy cooperation between the two countries but also redounded to the entry of Turkish construction companies to the Russian market at a time when other foreign competitors were unprepared or unwilling to exploit the dormant potential there.

As will be seen from Table 3.1, Turkey's natural gas imports from Russia increased steadily throughout the years. Besides, Russia was Turkey's sole provider until 1994. In that year Turkey started buying natural gas from Algeria to diversify its suppliers and reduce dependence on Russia. Nevertheless, the lion's share of profits from Turkish gas market still went to the Russian treasury as the natural gas transportation from Algeria was limited.

The Intergovernmental Agreement that was signed on December 15, 1997, during Russian Prime Minister Chernomyrdin's[1] visit to Turkey constituted another landmark in energy collaboration between Moscow and Ankara. The project called Blue Stream envisaged sending Russian natural gas to Turkey directly via a pipeline that would pass under the Black Sea. The new pipeline would supplement the existing western route which passed through Ukraine, Moldova, Romania and Bulgaria. The current long direction was making the gas more expensive and Turkey continually complained about gas being illicitly siphoned off while being shipped through Ukraine and Moldova. A direct pipeline between the two countries might solve these problems.

The total length of the conduit accounted for 1,213 km and it went at a record depth of 2,150 m below the sea. The pipeline started from Izobilnoye gas plant in southern Russia, ran to Dzhugba on the Black Sea, and then under the Black Sea to the Turkish port of Samsun. After Samsun, the Blue Stream continued towards its final destination Ankara (Devlet 2005, 76). On December 30, 2002, a protocol-signing ceremony for the Blue Stream commissioning took place in Durusu, near Samsun, and on February 20, 2003 the first Russian natural gas was transmitted to Turkey via the new pipeline (Gazprom 2008).

The Blue Stream gas pipeline came up against a lot of domestic and external criticism. Turkish critics stated that the project would lead to a

Table 3.1 Natural gas transportation by years (1987–2015) (million cubic meters)

Years	Russia	Iran	Azerbaijan	Algeria	Nigeria	Spot LNG
1987	433	—	—	—	—	—
1988	1,136	—	—	—	—	—
1989	2,986	—	—	—	—	—
1990	3,246	—	—	—	—	—
1991	4,031	—	—	—	—	—
1992	4,430	—	—	—	—	—
1993	4,952	—	—	—	—	—
1994	4,957	—	—	418	—	—
1995	5,560	—	—	1,058	—	—
1996	5,524	—	—	2,436	—	—
1997	6,574	—	—	3,300	—	—
1998	6,549	—	—	2,766	—	579
1999	8,698	—	—	2,964	69	300
2000	10,082	—	—	3,594	704	—
2001	10,928	114	—	3,627	1,197	—
2002	11,574	660	—	3,721	1,139	—
2003	12,460	3,461	—	3,795	1,107	—
2004	14,102	3,497	—	3,182	1,016	—
2005	17,524	4,248	—	3,786	1,013	—
2006	19,316	5,594	—	4,132	1,100	79
2007	22,762	6,054	1,258	4,205	1,396	167
2008	23,159	4,113	4,580	4,148	1,017	333
2009	19,473	5,252	4,960	4,487	903	781
2010	17,576	7,765	4,521	3,906	1,189	3,079
2011	25,406	8,190	3,806	4,156	1,248	1,069
2012	26,491	8,215	3,354	4,076	1,322	2,464
2013	26,212	8,730	4,245	3,917	1,274	892
2014	26,975	8,932	6,074	4,179	1,414	1,689
2015	26,783	7,826	6,169	3,916	1,240	2,493

Source: "Natural Gas Transportation, Facilities and Trade," BOTAŞ, accessed June 4, 2008, http://www.botas.gov.tr/eng/activities/ng_ttt.asp, 2010 Yılı Sektör Raporu (Ankara: BOTAŞ, 2011), 7, Doğal Gaz Piyasası 2013 Yılı Sektör Raporu (Ankara: EPDK, 2014), 20, Doğal Gaz Piyasası 2014 Yılı Sektör Raporu (Ankara: EPDK, 2015), 6, and Doğal Gaz Piyasası 2015 Yılı Sektör Raporu (Ankara: EPDK, 2016), 6.

parlous Turkish dependency on Russian energy sources and that Russia would use this infirmity as a wildcard to outsmart Turkey in the Caucasus and Central Asia. They also pointed out allegations of graft regarding the construction of the Turkish part of the pipeline. The USA also talked about the drawbacks of Turkey getting too ingrained with Russian gas imports (Bacik 2001, 89) and propounded the building of Trans-Caspian Gas Pipeline which would sideline Russia.

The project of natural gas imports from Turkmenistan through a submarine pipeline had been suggested by Washington in 1996. The project was activated on October 29, 1998, with the signing of a framework agreement between Turkey and Turkmenistan according to which Turkmenistan would deliver 30 billion m^3 of gas per year, 16 billion m^3 of which would be used in Turkey and the remainder would be transported to Europe (BOTAŞ 2008). On February 19, 1999, the Turkmen government entered into an agreement with General Electric and Bechtel Group for a feasibility study and on August 6, Shell joined the consortium ("Conference on Natural Gas" 2002, 77). Meanwhile, Turkey and Turkmenistan agreed on a commercial agreement on May 21, 1999 and this was followed by the signature of an intergovernmental declaration by Turkey, Turkmenistan, Azerbaijan and Georgia during the İstanbul OSCE Summit on November 18, 1999.

The Trans-Caspian Gas Pipeline project appealed to Turkey for two primary reasons. The project proposed the construction of a pipeline from Turkmenistan to Turkey running in parallel to the BTC crude oil pipeline until it joined the Eastern Anatolia natural gas transmission line near Erzurum ("Conference on Natural Gas" 2002, 79). Such a pipeline that transmitted natural gas to Europe through Turkish territory by circumventing both Russia and Iran would earn Turkey a distinct advantage in its regional rivalry with these countries. Moreover, the grave economic crisis in Russia that erupted in the summer of 1998 raised question marks in the minds of the Turkish policy-makers about the actualization of the Blue Stream gas pipeline.

Turkmenistan embraced the project wholeheartedly as it would reduce the country's dependence on Russia as the major export channel. Some of the gas reserves (about 20 billion m^3) of Turkmenistan were exported via Russia to Western countries and Ukraine, although Turkmenistan had been complaining with high fees imposed by the Russian government for the transit of its gas through the Russian pipeline (Tricarico 2001).

The possible construction of a rival pipeline to Blue Stream alarmed Russia. Moscow, while opposing the Trans-Caspian Gas Pipeline by indicating the unresolved legal status of the Caspian Sea, precipitated its efforts to find sponsors to finance the Blue Stream. In February 1999, Gazprom and the Italian ENI signed a Memorandum of Understanding for joint participation in the Blue Stream project implementation. On November 16, 1999, the two companies registered a special-purpose Russian–Italian entity, Blue Stream Pipeline B.V., on a parity basis in the Netherlands (Gazprom 2008). One week later, on November 23, 1999, the Russian–Italian joint venture signed a 1.7 billion dollar contract in Moscow with an international consortium headed by Saipem S.p.A., part of the Italian ENI Group, Bouygues Offshore SA, Katran-K, Mitsui & Co, Sumitomo Corp. and Itoshu Corporation to build the underwater section of the Blue Stream project (Tricarico 2001). These agreements removed Turkish qualms about financial viability of the scheme.

The running into snags on the Trans-Caspian Gas Pipeline also played into the hands of the proponents of the Blue Stream pipeline. Azerbaijan and Turkmenistan disagreed over ownership of the Caspian Sea resources, and Turkmenistan wanted Azerbaijan to pay gas debts from the early 1990s, although these were probably incurred by Azeri private firms. Moreover, the Turkmen state closed its embassy in Baku as a sign of its displeasure. On top of these, discovery of rich gas resources in Shah Deniz gas field of Azerbaijan in 1999 led to a loss of appetite for the Trans-Caspian Gas Pipeline on the Azerbaijani side.

There were also strong indications that in Turkey Blue Stream had a clique of advocates that was composed of owners of big construction conglomerates who were engaged in business activities in Russia, oil and gas executives from Turkish state petroleum pipeline company BOTAŞ, officials from the Turkish Energy Ministry and leading members of the coalition partner Motherland Party. Later, charges were also levelled against Deputy Prime Minister and Minister of State Mesut Yılmaz who also headed the Motherland Party, for lobbying in favor of Blue Stream in order to help his construction magnate cronies to secure deals in Russia and awarding the contract to build pipeline's Turkish section to his associates without a tender.[2]

With the signature of a protocol between Turkey and Russia regarding taxation of the Blue Stream pipeline project on November 27, 1999, it became clear that Russian gas won over the Turkmen one (Republic of Turkey Ministry of Foreign Affairs 1999). This gave rise to a strain in relations between Turkey and Turkmenistan and with shelving of the Trans-Caspian Gas Pipeline project; Ashgabat was compelled to sign a treaty with Russia to sell its gas to this country.

The amount of natural gas Turkey bought from Russia has mounted up over the years with the opening of the Blue Stream line in 2003.

Bearing in mind that reliance on a single supplier may leave the country in the lurch especially in the winter season in the case of a possible fall out with Moscow, Ankara had stepped up its exertion toward diversifying natural gas vendors and started to buy natural gas from Nigeria in 1999, Iran in 2001 and Azerbaijan in 2007. Furthermore, in December 2015 shortly after the escalation of the plane crisis with Russia, Turkey signed a Memorandum of Understanding with Qatar to purchase LNG from that country, thus expanding its list of natural gas suppliers. However, despite diversification efforts, Russia still ranks first in natural gas exports to Turkey as it has provided 59 percent of Turkey's natural gas need as of May 2016 (EPDK 2016, 3).

Natural gas exchange between Turkey and Russia did not encounter any interruptions during the political strife between the two countries. Geographical proximity and supply guarantee enabled Russia to come out as the best alternative for natural gas procurement for Turkey. Iran's sporadic cutting off gas supplies in the middle of the winter on the basis of domestic consumption needs and technical problems demonstrate that it is not a credible supplier. Natural gas procured from Azerbaijan, Algeria and Nigeria does not satisfy the local demand in full. Finally, Qatari gas is yet to be considered as a serious option taking into account the storage capacity of Turkey (Sheikh 2016). There exist currently only two underground storage facilities in Silivri and Değirmenköy and the third one is under construction in Tuz Gölü. Russia, on the other hand, did not suspend natural gas distribution to Turkey for a day (President of Russia 2016) as it could not afford to give up on its second largest customer especially when energy prices and profits of Gazprom were receding considerably.

Turkey in the past also supported alternative natural gas projects such as Nabucco, conceived to reduce European dependence on Russian natural gas by exploiting the reserves in Azerbaijan, Kazakhstan, Turkmenistan, and maybe in Iraq and Iran. The natural gas extracted from these source countries was to be transported via Turkey through Bulgaria, Romania and Hungary to Austria. Although the Intergovernmental Agreement for the proposed project was signed in Ankara on July 13, 2009, none of the mentioned prospective suppliers affirmed their intention of being involving in the project. The Nabucco project was shelved in June 2013 after Azerbaijan declared that it would inaugurate the Trans–Anatolian Natural Gas Pipeline Project which would replace Nabucco by carrying the Azerbaijani gas to the Western Europe through using Turkish, Greek and Albanian territory.

Despite Turkey's buoying up of the Nabucco project for some time, it became clear that the country was not intending to put all its eggs in one basket when Turkish Premier Erdoğan disclosed, at the time of Russian Prime Minister Putin's working trip to Turkey on August 6, 2009, that Ankara gave its consent to the construction of South Stream gas pipeline,[3] which was considered as a rival mission to Nabucco, via Turkey's economic zone (Government of the Russian Federation 2009). However, South Stream shared a similar fate with Nabucco and was cancelled following Bulgaria's withdrawal from the project in December 2014. Bulgaria's change of heart was attributed to the pressure the EU imposed on the tiny Balkan state stemming from Brussel's showdown with Moscow over Ukraine (Gloystein and Zhdannikov 2014).

Russian President Putin came up with a new gas pipeline project in the joint news conference he held with his Turkish counterpart Erdoğan on December 1, 2014 after revealing that the Bulgarian route was off the table. Putin stated that Russia might consider building another south European gas pipeline, this time on Turkish territory, which would reach Europe traversing Greece (President of Russia 2014). Preliminary agreement regarding the construction of Turkish Stream, as the Russian side dubbed the proposed gas pipeline, was signed on May 7, 2015, in the course of Gazprom Chairman Alexey Miller's meeting with the Turkish Minister of Energy and Natural Resources. Taner Yıldız in Ankara (Gazprom 2015). Although the project was suspended on December 3, 2015 following the rift between Ankara and Moscow, Russian Energy Minister Alexander Novak declared on July 29, 2016, approximately one month after the reconciliation between the two countries, that the Turkish Stream was becoming increasingly attractive for Russia due to rising cost of gas transmission through Ukraine ("Novak: Turkish Stream" 2016). If the project comes into existence, it will constitute another huge milestone in the energy cooperation between Turkey and Russia in the post-Cold War period.

In addition to being Turkey's chief natural gas provider, Russia also provides oil and electricity to Turkey. Russia supplied nearly 18 percent of Turkey's oil requirement in 2015, thus becoming the second biggest oil supplier of Turkey after Iraq (EPDK 2015, 1). Moscow started to export electricity to Turkey through the subsidiary of Inter RAO UES, TGR Enerji, starting from August 2010. Total electricity supply comes to 12 million kilowatt hours a month with a maximum capacity of up to 30 megawatts. In order to optimize supplies during the spring and summer period, the company delivers electricity from Georgia and during the autumn–winter period—via transit from Russia. Electricity from Russia is supplied through Georgian territory via the Batumi-Khopa line (Office of the Commercial Counsellor of Turkish Embassy in Moscow 2010, 6).

Another milestone in Turkish–Russian energy cooperation had been the signing of an intergovernmental agreement between the two countries on May 12, 2010, at the time of Russian President Medvedev's visit to Turkey, with which Russia obtained the right to construct and operate a nuclear power plant at the Akkuyu site in Mersin via the establishment of a subsidiary whose total shares would be owned by its state company Rosatom. Turkey will purchase electricity generated in the nuclear unit for 15 years and it will also be granted 20 percent of the profit that will be earned from the plant (Kışlalı 2010).

Construction and contracting services

The construction industry has become another locomotive sector between Turkey and Russia in the post-Cold War period. The Unification Treaty of Former East and West Germany signed on July 1, 1990, between the Federal German Government and Russia, which stipulated the return of 100,000 Russian soldiers based in Former East Germany to their home country, initiated the Turkish contractors' adventure in Russia. The German government undertook the financing of the housing projects to be constructed for these soldiers and their families. Fifteen thousand out of a total 46,000 housing units were built by Turkish companies such as Baytur, Enka, Gama, Mesa, Tekfen, Tekser, and Yapı Merkezi. The total value of these military housing projects equaled two and a half billion Deutschmarks (Republic of Turkey Prime Ministry Undersecretariat of Foreign Trade 2006).

During the following years Turkish construction corporations were heavily engaged in construction, restoration and renovation of public buildings, shopping malls, business and trade centers, hotels, guesthouses and restaurants, residential buildings, industrial facilities, hospitals and rehabilitation centers, historical, architectural and exhibition complexes and schools and educational centers in various parts of Russia. At the initial phase, Turkish companies worked on assiduously and perseveringly to foster close relations with government authorities and municipalities. These efforts paid off in the long term and they obtained lucrative bids from state-controlled corporations and private firms by overrunning foreign competitors. By June 30, 2016 Turkish companies had completed construction projects in Russia that were worth 64 billion dollars (Republic of Turkey Moscow Embassy 2016). Over three billion dollars' worth of these construction projects were completed in 2014 within the framework of the Sochi Winter Olympics project (President of Russia 2014). Russia ranked first with 20 percent share in terms of the total number of projects finished by Turkish firms abroad.

Russia's decision to prohibit Turkish companies or firms controlled by Turkish citizens (with some exemptions) from performing construction, engineering and architectural work in the country, along with the ban on recruitment of new Turkish employees from January 1, 2016, inflicted a heavy blow on the Turkish construction sector. The contracting projects in Russia had created significant business opportunities for Turkish workers. The number of Turkish construction workforce in Russia was about 10,000 (İlhan 2009) and they were serving in construction sites dispersed in various locations of Russia. This became another lose-lose situation for both countries. While the Turkish companies and employees were deprived of a profitable market, Russia started to feel the absence of long-standing Turkish firms which were renowned with their high-quality work and skilled construction personnel ("Impact of Sanctions against Turkey" 2015). The resumption of close economic ties between Turkey and Russia is expected to have a positive impact on the construction sector as well.

The Russian construction companies entered into contracting activities in Turkey as well but their fields of activity were more limited and mostly concentrated on infrastructural work and construction and renovation of industrial facilities. Technopromexport participated to the building of Orhaneli Thermal Power Reactor. A joint consortium of Technostroyexport, Turkish Erg İnşaat and Swiss ABB, Sulzer Hydro, Hydro Vevey and Stucky Companies started the construction of Deriner Dam near the Black Sea town of Artvin in April 1998 ("Çoruh'a Altın Kelepçe" 1998). Energomachexport and Turkish Baytur and Özdemir won the tender for building of Torul Dam and hydroelectric power station near the Black Sea city of Gümüşhane in October 2000 ("Torul Barajı" 2000). Stroytransgaz completed the Turkish section (Samsun-Ankara) of the Blue Stream pipeline in 2001 (Stroytransgaz 2013). SMU-4, in partnership with Turkish Tepe İnşaat, finished the Kayseri part of Sivas-Kayseri natural gas pipeline in 2002 (Özaslan and Şeftalici 2002, 206).

Technostroyexport and Turkish Tekser cooperated in the electrification of Turkish railways in addition to the building of bridges and dams (Kolobov, Kornilov, and Özbay 2006, 51). Transstroy and Turkish Hazinedaroğlu and Ünüvar Consortium constructed the 2.2 km-long light rapid transit system in Eminönü-Kabataş and 16.3 km-long light transit system in the Sultançiftliği-Edirnekapı-Vezneciler regions of İstanbul including all electro-mechanical works (Hazinedaroğlu 2013; Ünüvar 2013). Moreover, Russian companies were involved in upgrading of the İskenderun metal hardware plant, provided engineering services for the gas storage facility installations and erected an aqueduct within the context of İstanbul Melen project (Şen 2003, 5).

Mutual investments

The Turkish capital has been pouring into Russia since the late 1990s through big Turkish conglomerates and medium-sized Turkish firms. By the end of the first quarter of 2015, Turkish investments in the country had exceeded 10 billion dollars (DEİK 2015a, 2), centering on banking, consumer durables, fast-moving consumer goods, retail, media and manufacturing sectors. There existed approximately 3,000 Turkish companies in Russia before the plane incident of November 2015 (Republic of Turkey Moscow Embassy 2016) and around 200 of them left the country after the crisis according to unofficial estimates (Winning 2016). In recent years Turkish companies have also started to shift their attention from Moscow and St. Petersburg to smaller cities and provinces such as Ivanovo, Tver and Vladimir where they took advantage of cheaper raw materials, a less costly workforce and incentives from the Russian state (DEİK 2005, 14; Tuvay 2008, 16–7).

Leading Turkish conglomerates such as Anadolu Group, Doğan Holding, Eczacıbaşı Holding, Koç Holding, Zorlu Holding as well as significant industrial corporations such as Enka and Şişecam have realized high-scale investments in Russia in the post-Cold War era. Ramenka was founded in Moscow in 1997 as a joint undertaking of Koç and Enka. Ramenka hypermarkets and shopping malls sold European and Russian brands of foods, beverages, clothings, cleaning products, textile goods and small household appliances. The Koç Group's other remarkable investment in Russia was its first facility built overseas, the Beko refrigerator and washing machine plant in Kirzhach, Vladimir which started production in October 2006. The plant celebrated its millionth product in November 2008, and it was dubbed the 'Company of the Year' in Russia and received the award for 'the company with highest quality products' ("Beko'dan Rusya'da" 2008).

Anadolu Group established Moscow Efes Brewery in 1999 in partnership with the European Bank for Reconstruction and Development and City Government of Moscow. In that same year, the firm launched the Stary-Melnik beer brand and production commenced in the malt production facility in Moscow, adjacent to Moscow Efes Brewery. Currently, the company has ten production units in Russia and holds

15 percent market share (Anadolu Efes 2016). Russia ranks first in Anadolu Efes' all beer operations in terms of sales volume.

Şişecam put into operation in June 2002, in the Vladimir region of Russia, the first furnace of the Ruscam Gorohovets Plant with a capacity of 90,000 tons/year with the purpose of fulfilling the demand for high-quality beer bottles of the country's ever-growing beer market. Paşabahçe, the glassware subsidiary of Şişecam, made its first foreign investment in 2003 and took over 100 percent shares of the Posuda manufacturing glassware in Nizhny Novgorod from Bor Glassworks. In 2004, Şişecam purchased the Pokrovsky Plant located near St. Petersburg which specialized in the glass-packaging business and Anadolu Cam became a partner of the Balkum Sand Plant in Balahna. Anadolu Cam glass-packaging investment in Ufa was completed in 2005 and in the same year the first foreign prestige shop of Paşabahçe was opened in Moscow (Şişecam 2009). Şişecam also commenced glass-packaging investments in Kirishi, Kuban, Novosibirsk and St. Petersburg in the years 2007 and 2008 (DEİK 2008, 65).

Zorlu Holding entered the Russian market with the foundation of Vestel CIS in November 2003 in Alexandrov as the first foreign company to manufacture TV sets in the country. A fire that broke out on November 14, 2005 completely destroyed the television plant. Vestel CIS carried on its activities in Russia with the washing machine and refrigerator factories which came on stream in 2006 (Vestel 2013). In May 2010, the Company inaugurated its LCD TV production unit (Başlamış 2010). Zorlu Energy, another subsidiary of the Group, constructed the Tereshkovo and Kojukhovo electric power plants in Moscow through its subsidiary Rosmiks ("Zorlu Enerji Moskova'da" 2011).

In 2007, *Hürriyet*, the flagship newspaper of the Doğan Holding, purchased 67.3 percent shares of the Trader Media East Corporation, which provided print and online classified advertising services in Russia, CIS, Baltics, Balkans and Eastern European region (Trader Media East 2013). In December 2008, Eczacıbaşı Building Products Group laid the foundation for the establishment of a ceramic production and vitrification plant in Serpukhov ("Eczacıbaşı'ndan Rusya'ya Yatırım" 2008) and in September 2014, the company opened a second factory which would specialize in ceramic health devices ("Rusya'da Dev Yatırım" 2014).

There exist also a handful of Turkish banks that have stepped into Russia during the early and mid-1990s following the footprints of the Turkish entrepreneurs. Yapı Kredi and Ziraat Bank established their Moscow branches in 1993, Garanti Bank in 1995 and Credit Europe in

1997. The customer base of these banks was mostly made up of small and medium-sized enterprises of the Russian economy and prominent Turkish corporations active in the Russian market. In the late 2000s, Turkish banks have entered into partnerships or acquired Russian banks to consolidate their position in Russia. With 51 percent Turkish capital, ProCommerce Bank was founded in Moscow in mid-2006 by a group of Turkish and Russian investors. The bank provides commercial banking services and credit to small and medium-sized firms and individuals doing business in Russia (Artemis Sümer, Turkish Ministry of Foreign Affairs, correspondence with the author, October 22, 2010). In October 2010, Turkey's biggest private bank, Türkiye İş Bankası, acquired a 100 percent interest of Russian Bank Sofia with the objective of serving Turkish firms which were operating in Russia and were clients of Türkiye İş Bankası ("Turkish Lender Isbank" 2010).

The medium-sized Turkish enterprises realized remarkable investments in Russia as well. Eroğlu Group's denim products company Colin's Jeans which opened its first store in Moscow in 1995 augmented the number of its shops in Russia to 220 (Eroğlu Holding 2016) and expanded its wholesale and retail operations in 94 locations of the country. Denkateks purchased a textile plant in Ivanovo in 2009 that dated from the Czarist empire but closed down after the end of the Soviet Union and reopened it as a home textile factory ("Ivanova'nın Antalya'sı" 2011). In May 2009 Kalekim, the prominent construction chemical producer of Turkey, inaugurated a ceramic pasting and isolation mortar production unit in Serpukhov ("Kalekim Bölgesel Liderliği Hedefliyor" 2009). In September 2010, Turkey's air carrier Atlasjet and the government of Russia's Omsk region declared that they would set up a joint company to set up a regional airline and construct an international airport in Omsk ("Russia's Omsk Region" 2010). In October 2010, DYO, one of Turkey's leading dye companies, and whose products has been on the Russian market for 12 years through dealers, started production in its facility in Krasnodar ("Turkish Dye Company" 2010). Boydak Holding, a conglomerate which mainly operates in furniture, textile, chemistry, marketing, iron-steel, logistics, energy sectors, declared in March 2011 its purchase of two furniture factories in Russia and Ukraine from the Polish Forte at 20 million dollars ("Boydak Ukrayna ve Rusya'da" 2011).

Russian investments in Turkey have exhibited a conspicuous surge since mid-2000s. At June 30, 2016, the value of Russian businesses in Turkey surpassed 10 billion dollars (Republic of Turkey Moscow Embassy 2016). There exist 1,947 Russian firms in Turkey, constituting 4 percent of all foreign capital companies in the Turkish market

(DEİK 2015b). Russian capital came into Turkey in the form of acquisitions and through partnerships with local Turkish companies mostly in the fields of energy, technology and telecommunications, banking and manufacturing.

Gazprom has emerged as an important player both in supply and distribution of natural gas to the Turkish market since early 2000s. The firm took hold of a 40 percent stake in Bosphorus Gaz Corporation via its German subsidiary Zarubezhgaz Management und BeteiligungsgesellschaftmbH (ZMB) and its export arm Gazexport in 2004 (Bosphorus Gaz Corporation 2006). Gazprom currently possesses 70 percent of the shares of Bosphorus Gaz and the company was granted to sell and distribute 1,750 million m^3 of the imported Russian gas, which made it the second biggest natural gas importer company of Turkey after BOTAŞ (Bosphorus Gaz Corporation 2013). Moreover, the subsidiary of Gazprom, Gazprombank, purchased a 26 percent stake in January 2012 in Avrasya Gaz, another gas trading company in Turkey and later on increased its share in the firm to 60 percent (Ersoy 2012).

Lukoil signed an agreement with Akpet, a petroleum and petroleum products distributor that had 693 gas filling stations and a market share of 5 percent in July 2008 to gain 100 percent interests of the company (Lukoil 2008). Akpet, which belonged to Aytemiz Group, was Turkey's sixth largest fuel oil distribution firm as well as the second biggest enterprise in terms of number of stations and the third largest oil storage corporation (Daly 2008b).

Inter RAO Turkey Energy Holding, an affiliate of Russian energy giant Inter RAO UES Group purchased 90 percent share of Trakya Elektrik which possessed power purchase and gas sales licensing rights in Turkey in December 2012 from AEI Energy for 67.5 million dollars (Inter RAO UES 2012).

In November 2005 Altimo, an affiliate of Alfa Group Consortium, a large financial-industrial conglomerate in Russia, finalized a series of transactions totaling 3.3 billion dollars with Çukurova Group, resulting in Alfa's acquisition of 13.2 percent share of Turkcell, the leading telecommunications company in Turkey. In 2011 Russia's number one search engine Yandex launched its operations in Turkey by establishing an office in İstanbul (Yandex 2011). CROC; one of the leading information technology firms of Russia acquired a majority stake in Turkish NGN in 2013 which, similar to itself, specialized in systems integration ("Rusya'nın En Büyük BT" 2013).

Sberbank, the largest bank of Russia and Eastern Europe, carried out its largest acquisition in the bank's history in June 2012 by buying

DenizBank, Turkey's eighth biggest bank in terms of asset size, from Belgian Dexia Group for 3.53 billion dollars (Sberbank 2012). Russian investment bank Renaissance Capital stepped into the Turkish market in March 2012 after completing acquisition of Mira Securities (Renaissance Capital 2013).

In May 2007, Russian Magnitogorsk Iron and Steel Works (MMK) and the Turkish Atakaş signed an agreement to jointly build a new steel plant in Turkey. The new plant would occupy two sites, with main production facilities located in İskenderun, and a second site near in Gebze. It planned to produce about 2.4 million tons of flat products from steel scrap and metalized raw materials (MMK 2008). In March 2011, MMK signed an agreement with the Atakaş family and purchased the shares under its control, thus becoming the sole owner of the investment (MMK 2011).

In September 2007, Segezha Packaging, world's second largest industrial paper sack manufacturing company that belonged to Russian ILP Group, announced that it had acquired the cement sack operations of Işıklar Ambalaj, with two sack plants which were located in Elazığ and İzmir (Segezha Packaging 2007). In July 2010 Mechel, one of the leading Russian mining and steel companies, purchased for 3 million dollars whole shares of the Turkish steel company Ramateks which specialized in the distribution of carbon, alloy and stainless steel (Donat 2010). Russia's biggest manufacturer of commercial vehicles, GAZ Group in partnership with Turkish Mersa Automotiv, established a company in Sakarya in 2012 for production of light trucks ("Turkey: GAZ Teams with Mersa" 2012).

Growing, diversifying and strengthening economic relations between Turkey and Russia in the post-Cold War period demonstrated that the two countries have become increasingly significant for each other. Turkey's natural gas imports from Russia continued to be the most important item in the bilateral trade. Russia preserved its top place as Turkey's number one natural gas provider among many competitors such as Iran, Azerbaijan, Algeria and Nigeria. It started to satisfy Turkey's oil and electricity needs as well. Electricity purchases from Russia will also augment with Russia's completion of Turkey's first nuclear power plant in Akkuyu.

Reciprocal investments between Turkey and Russia, despite falling far behind the investments carried out by European companies, demonstrated an ascending trend all over the years. While Turkish firms overwhelmingly invested in construction, fast-moving consumer goods, consumer durables and manufacturing sectors in Russia, Russian companies in Turkey focused to a large extent on energy, financial services, technology and telecommunications and manufacturing businesses.

This part of the study attested to the fact that growing and deepening economic ties have been at the top of the agenda of Turkish–Russian relations in most of the post-Cold War era. The increasing bilateral trade, strengthening energy bonds, and various mutual investments have brought the business worlds of Turkey and Russia closer together and paved the way for dialogue, interaction and cooperation on the political sphere. Although it is not possible to relegate to the background the security issues in the relationship, as became evident when the crisis broke out over Syria, economic matters too gained considerable prominence in the Turkish–Russian equation. Furthermore, some representatives of the Turkish and Russian business worlds have contributed to a significant extent to the restoration of political ties between Turkey and Russia by shuttling back and forth between the two presidents in order to reopen channels of communication and dialogue in the most serious bilateral political dispute ever since the Cold War. So it is safe to say that it is now impossible to set aside the economic factor while examining the Turkish–Russian intercourse.

Notes

1 Before assuming the post of premier, Chernomyrdin worked as the chairman of Gazprom, the Russian state natural gas monopoly and also the deputy prime minister in charge of fuel and energy.
2 These allegations were investigated by the State Security Court in Ankara, and several high ranking functionaries of the Ministry of Energy were put into prison. This White Energy inquisition also led to the resignation of Energy Minister Cumhur Ersümer from his post on April 26, 2001. See Amberin Zaman, "Corruption Scandal Threatens to Sink Blue Stream Pipeline Project," *Business&Economics*, May 31, 2001 and Robert M. Cutler, "The Blue Stream Gas Project: Not a Pipe-Dream Anymore," *CACI Analyst*, January 8, 2001.
3 The projected pipeline was envisaged to transport Russian natural gas to the Black Sea to Bulgaria and further to Italy and Austria.

References

AA, "Turkish Dye Company Starts Production in Russia." 2010. October 21.
Amos, Howard. 2016. "Oil Price Woe Pushes Russian Economy to 3.7 percent Contraction in 2015, Hits Country's Poorest." *International Business Times*, January 25.

Anadolu Efes. 2016. "Operations, Russia." *Anadolu Efes*. Accessed August 3, 2016. http://www.anadoluefes.com/index.php?gdil=in&gsayfa=op&galtsayfa=operasyonlardetay&gicsayfa=rusya&gislem=&gbilgi=/.
Arslan, Elif Ünal. 2005. "Russian Ambassador Says Cooperation Intact Despite Fruit Fly Trouble." *Turkish Daily News*, June 10.
Automotive World, "Turkey: GAZ Teams with Mersa for Local Assembly." 2012. July 9.
Bacik, Gökhan. 2001. "The Blue Stream Project, Energy Cooperation and Conflicting Interests." *Turkish Studies* 2(2): 85–93.
Başlamış, Cenk. 2010. "Rusya'ya 15 Milyon Dolarlık Vestel Yatırımı." *Milliyet*, May 29.
Bosphorus Gaz Corporation. 2006. "Energy and Gas Report." *Bosphorus Gaz Corporation*. Accessed August 3, 2013. http://www.bosphorusgaz.com/fileadmin/bosphorusgaz/documents/gas_report_nocontents.pdf/.
Bosphorus Gaz Corporation. 2013. "Profile." *Bosphorus Gaz Corporation*. Accessed August 3, 2013. http://www.bosphorusgaz.com/sirketimiz-2/profil.
BOTAŞ. 1984. "Gazexport-Rusya Federasyonu ile Doğal Gaz Alım-Satım Anlaşması (Batı)." *BOTAŞ*. Accessed June 3, 2008. http://www.botas.gov.tr/faliyetler/antlasmalar/rusya.asp/.
BOTAŞ. 2008. "Türkmenistan ile Doğal Gaz Alım-Satım Anlaşması." BOTAŞ. Accessed October 26, 2008. http://www.botas.gov.tr/.
Central Bank of Turkey. 2016. "Ödemeler Dengesi İstatistikleri." *Central Bank of Turkey*. Accessed July 31, 2016. http://www.tcmb.gov.tr/wps/wcm/connect/TCMB+TR/TCMB+TR/Main+Menu/Istatistikler/Odemeler+Dengesi+ve+Ilgili+Istatistikler/Odemeler+Dengesi+Istatistikleri/Veri+Tablolar/.
Daly, John C.K. 2008a. "Does Turkish-Russian Agricultural Dispute Have Underlying Causes?" *Eurasia Daily Monitor* 5(111), June 11.
Daly, John C.K. 2008b. "Lukoil and Turkey." *Eurasia Daily Monitor* 5(150), August 6.
DEİK. 2005. *Turkish Business in the BSEC Region: Direct Investments, Contracting Services, Prospects for Cooperation*. İstanbul: DEİK.
DEİK. 2008. *Rusya İş Yapma Rehberi*. İstanbul: DEİK.
DEİK. 2013. "About *DEİK*: Purpose." *DEİK*. Accessed July 23, 2013. http://www.deik.org.tr/pages/EN/DEIK_DeikHakkinda.aspx?IKID=10/.
DEİK. 2015a. *Türkiye-Rusya İş Forumu 22 Nisan 2015 Sonuç Raporu*. Antalya: DEİK.
DEİK. 2015b. "31.12.2015 Tarihi İtibariyle Türkiye'de Faaliyette Bulunan Yabancı Sermayeli Firmalar Listesi." *DEİK*. Accessed August 3, 2016. https://www.deik.org.tr/6499/31_12_2015_Tarihi_ percentC4 percentB0tibariyle_T percentC3 percentBCrkiye_de_Faaliyette_Bulunan_Yabanc percentC4 percentB1_Sermayeli_Firmalar_Listesi.html/.
Devlet, Nadir. 2005. "Turkey's Energy Policy in the Next Decade." *Perceptions (Journal of International Affairs)* 9(4): 71–90.
Donat, İrfan. 2010. "Rus Mechel, Ramateks'i 3 Milyon Dolara Satın Aldı." *Sabah*, July 12.

Dünya, "Beko'dan Rusya'da 1 Milyonuncu Ürün Gururu." 2008. November 27.
Dünya, "Rusya ile Ticarette Sadece Kusurlu Firma Ceza Alacak." 2009. April 29.
Dünya, "Torul Barajı ve HES İhalesi Tamam." 2000. October 2.
EPDK. 2015. *Aralık 2015 Petrol Piyasası Sektör Raporu*. Ankara: EPDK.
EPDK. 2016. *Mayıs 2016 Doğal Gaz Piyasası Sektör Raporu*. Ankara: EPDK.
Eroğlu Holding. 2016. "Rakamlarla Eroğlu." *Eroğlu Holding*. Accessed August 3, 2016. http://www.erogluholding.com/bizi-taniyin/rakamlarla-eroglu/.
Ersoy, Ercan. 2012. "Gazprombank Unit to Buy 26 percent of Trader Avrasya, Turkey Board Says." *Bloomberg*, January 3.
Gazprom. 2008. "About/Major Projects/Blue Stream/History." *Gazprom*. Accessed October 26, 2008. http://www.gazprom.com/eng/articles/article8895.shtml/.
Gazprom. 2015. "Alexey Miller and Taner Yildiz Address Turkish Stream." *Gazprom*. Accessed May 26, 2015. http://www.gazprom.com/press/news/2015/may/article226027/.
Gloystein, Henning, and Dmitry Zhdannikov. 2014. "Russia's South Stream Pipeline Falls Victim to Ukraine Crisis, Energy Rout." *Reuters*, December 2.
Government of the Russian Federation. 2009. "Prime Minister Vladimir Putin and his Turkish Counterpart Recep Tayyip Erdoğan Held a Joint News Conference on the Results of the Talks." *Government of the Russian Federation*. Accessed July 28, 2013. http://premier.gov.ru/eng/visits/world/123/3400.html/.
Haberrus, "Ivanova'nın Antalya'sı Çarların Tekstil Fabrikasını Canlandırdı." 2011. October 22.
Habertürk Ekonomi, "Eczacıbaşı'ndan Rusya'ya Yatırım." 2008. December 5.
Has, Kerim. 2016. "Türk-Rus İlişkilerinde 'Temkinli Normalleşme' Dönemi." 2016. *USAK*, July 2.
Hazinedaroğlu. 2013. "Hazinedaroğlu Group, Turkey." *Hazinedaroğlu*. Accessed July 30, 2013. http://www.hazinedaroglu-group.com/CountryDetail.aspx?CID=6/.
Hürriyet, "Çoruh'a Altın Kelepçe." 1998. April 27.
Hürriyet, "Zorlu Enerji Moskova'da Santral Açtı." 2011. November 14.
Inter RAO UES. 2012. "Inter RAO UES Group Completed Acquisition of a Power Generation Asset in Turkey." *Inter RAO UES*. Accessed August 4, 2013. http://www.interrao.ru/en/news/company/?ELEMENT_ID=3409/.
International Energy Agency, "Conference on Natural Gas Transit and Storage in Southeast Europe: An Opportunity to Diversify European Gas Supply?" *International Energy Agency* 2002: 73–86.
ITC Trade Map. 2016a. "List of Supplying Markets for the Product Imported by Russian Federation in 2015." *ITC Trade Map*. Accessed July 30, 2016. http://www.trademap.org/Country_SelProductCountry.aspx/.

ITC Trade Map. 2016b. "List of Importing Markets for the Product Exported by Russian Federation in 2015." *ITC Trade Map.* Accessed July 30, 2016. http://www.trademap.org/Country_SelProductCountry.aspx/.

İlhan, Leyla. 2009. "Müteahhitlerin Rusya'daki İşlerinde yüzde 50 Gerileme Var." *Dünya,* August 11.

Keohane, Robert O., and Joseph S. Nye Jr. 1977. *Power and Interdependence: World Politics in Transition.* Boston: Little Brown.

Kışlalı, Murat. 2010. "Rusya'ya Ödün Kar Payı İçin." *Cumhuriyet,* June 20.

Kolobov, Oleg A., Aleksandr A. Kornilov, and Fatih Özbay. 2006. *Çağdaş Türk-Rus İlişkileri: Sorunlar ve İşbirliği Alanları 1992–2005.* İstanbul: Tasam Yayınları.

Kommersant, "Turkish Lender Isbank Looking to Announce Acquisition of Bank Sofia in Days to Come." 2010. October 25.

Lukoil. 2008. "Lukoil Acquires Large Retail Assets in Turkey." *Lukoil.* Accessed August 4, 2013. http://www.lukoil.com/press.asp?div_id=1&id=2907/.

Milliyet, "Boydak Ukrayna ve Rusya'da İki Mobilya Fabrikası Satın Aldı." 2011. March 14.

Milliyet, "Kalekim Bölgesel Liderliği Hedefliyor." 2009. March 5.

MMK. 2008. "MMK is Making Headway with its Turkey Project." *MMK.* Accessed August 4, 2013. http://www.mmk.ru/eng/press/news/article.wbp?article-id=E4ADA29B-AC10-1016-01B1-FBF4553F4236/.

MMK. 2011. "OJSC Magnitogorsk Iron and Steel Works (MMK) Announces Signing of Share Purchase Agreement with View to Consolidate 100 percent shares of MMK Atakaş Metalürji Sanayi Ticaret ve Liman İşletmeciliği Anonim Şirketi." *MMK.* Accessed August 4, 2013. http://eng.mmk.ru/press_center/49267/.

Nacar, Pınar Çelik. 2016. "Russia Approaches Turkey to Reduce Food Prices." *Daily Sabah,* April 23.

Office of the Commercial Counsellor of Turkish Embassy in Moscow. 2010. *Aylık Raporlar-Ağustos.* Moscow: Turkish Embassy in Moscow/.

Official Gazette. 2008. "Türkiye Cumhuriyeti Gümrük Müsteşarlığı ile Rusya Federasyonu Federal Gümrük Servisi Arasında Gümrük İşlemlerinin Basitleştirilmesine İlişkin Protokol'un Onaylanması." *Official Gazette.* Accessed July 27, 2013. http://rega.basbakanlik.gov.tr/#/.

Özaslan, Metin, and Haluk Şeftalici. 2002. *Kayseri City Development Report.* Ankara: SPO Publications.

President of Russia. 2014. "News Conference Following State Visit to Turkey." *President of Russia.* Accessed May 26, 2015. http://eng.kremlin.ru/news/23322/.

President of Russia. 2016. "Meeting with Heads of International News Agencies." *President of Russia.* Accessed August 1, 2016. http://en.kremlin.ru/events/president/news/52183/.

Renaissance Capital. 2013. "About." *Renaissance Capital.* Accessed August 4, 2013. http://www.rencap.com/MENA/About/.

Republic of Turkey Ministry of Foreign Affairs. 1999. "Türkiye Cumhuriyeti Hükümeti ile Rusya Federasyonu Hükümeti Arasında Rus Doğal Gazının Karadeniz Altından Türkiye Cumhuriyeti'ne Sevkiyatına İlişkin Protokol." *Republic of Turkey Ministry of Foreign Affairs.* Accessed October 26, 2008. http://www.mfa.gov.tr/mfa_tr/PDF_Pool/showUAFile.aspx/.

Republic of Turkey Moscow Embassy. 2016. "Türkiye-Rusya Ekonomik ve Ticari İlişkileri." *Republic of Turkey Moscow Embassy.* Accessed August 2, 2016. http://moscow.emb.mfa.gov.tr/ShowInfoNotes.aspx?ID=219659/.

Republic of Turkey Prime Ministry Undersecretariat of Foreign Trade. 2006. "Rusya Federasyonu Müteahhitlik Hizmetleri Ülke Profili." *Republic of Turkey Prime Ministry Undersecretariat of Foreign Trade.* Accessed July 30, 2013. http://www.dtm.gov.tr/dtmadmin/upload/ANL/YurtDisiMuteahhitDb/ulkeler/rusya-mut.raporu.pdf/.

RIA Novosti, "Russia's Omsk Region and Turkey's Atlas Jet to Set Up Airline in Siberia." 2010. September 15.

Sabah, "Rusya'da Dev Yatırım." 2014. May 19.

Sberbank. 2012. "Sberbank Announces Agreement to Acquire 99.85 percent of DenizBank." *Sberbank.* Accessed August 4, 2013. http://sberbank.ru/en/presscenter/all/index.php?id114=11018517/.

Segezha Packaging. 2007. "Segezha Packaging Acquires Assets in Turkey." *Segezha Packaging.* Accessed August 4, 2013. http://www.segezha-packaging.com/page139.aspx?newsid139=12/.

Sheikh, Salman Rafi. 2016. "Turkey Can't Replace Russian Gas with Qatari LNG." *Asia Times,* April 1.

State Planning Organization. 1992. "Rusya Federasyonu Hükümeti ile Yapılan Ticari ve Ekonomik İşbirliği Konularında Türk-Rus Karma Ekonomik Komisyonu Kurulmasına İlişkin Anlaşma." *State Planning Organization.* Accessed July 23, 2013. http://www.dpt.gov.tr/dei/index.html/.

Stroytransgaz. 2013. "Completed Oil and Gas Construction Projects." *Stroytransgaz.* Accessed July 30, 2013. http://www.stroytransgaz.com/projects/turkey/samsun-ankara_gas_pipeline/.

Şen, Cihangir Gürkan. 2003. "Türk-Rus Ekonomik İlişkileri: Mevcut Durum, Sorunlar ve Perspektifler." *Stradigma* 7: 1–9.

Şisecam. 2009. "History." *Şisecam.* Accessed September 21, 2009. http://www.sisecam.com/history/chronology.html/.

TASS, "Novak: Turkish Stream Pipeline Becoming More Attractive." 2016. July 29.

TASS, "Turkey Loses $209 Million 2016 Due to Food Embargo – Ministry." 2016. July 28.

Tekerek, Tuğba, and Serkan Arman. 2008. "Ucuz Gübre ve Çin İlacı Domatesi Yaktı." *Milliyet,* June 12.

Thinkpol, "Impact of Sanctions against Turkey on Russia's Economy Divides Opinion." 2015. November 30.

Trader Media East. 2013. "About Us." *Trader Media East*. Accessed August 1, 2013. http://www.tmeast.com/tmeast/index.php?option=com_content&view=category&layout=blog&id=1&Itemid=13/.
Tricarico, Antonio. 2001. "The Blue Stream-Black Sea Gas Pipeline Project." *EcaWatch*, September.
Turk-Internet, "Rusya'nın En Büyük BT – Bilisim Teknolojileri Entegrasyon Şirketi CROC Türkiye Pazarına Giriyor." 2013. November 26.
Turkish Institute of Statistics. 2015. "Yıllara Göre Dış Ticaret Verileri." *Turkish Institute of Statistics*. Accessed May 26, 2015. http://www.tuik.gov.tr/VeriBilgi.do?tb_id=12&ust_id=4/.
Turkish Institute of Statistics. 2016a. "Ülkelere Göre Yıllık İhracat ve İthalat." *Turkish Institute of Statistics*. Accessed July 30, 2016. http://www.tuik.gov.tr/UstMenu.do?metod=temelist/.
Turkish Institute of Statistics. 2016b. "Dış Ticaret İstatistikleri Veri Tabanı." *Turkish Institute of Statistics*. Accessed July 30, 2016. https://biruni.tuik.gov.tr/disticaretapp/disticaret.zul?param1=4&param2=0&sitcrev=0&isicrev=0&sayac=5808/.
Tuvay, Burcu. 2008. "Rusya'da Gerçek Fırsatlar Moskova Dışında." *KOBİ Girisim*: 16–17.
Ünüvar. 2013. "Ünüvar Construction, Light Rail System Projects." *Ünüvar*. Accessed July 30, 2013. http://www.unuvarinsaat.com.tr/web/eng/raylisistem.aspx?SecilenProjeNo=25/.
Vestel. 2013. "Vestel Group of Companies-Vestel CIS Ltd." *Zorlu Group*. Accessed July 31, 2013. http://www.zorlu.com.tr/EN/GRUP/ves_cis.asp/.
Winning, Alexander. 2016. "Turkish Firms in Russia Struggle as Diplomatic Row Rages." *Reuters*, March 30.
Yandex. 2011. "Yandex Launches in Turkey." *Yandex*. Accessed August 4, 2013. http://company.yandex.com/press_center/press_releases/2011/2011-09-20.xml/.

Conclusion

This book examined the political, economic and military dimensions of Turkish–Russian relations in the post-Cold War era by taking into account three important changes that the relationship has undergone throughout this period. While complex interdependency theory was of significant use to figure out the underlying causes of the first two shifts in the bilateral association, it needed to be supplemented with the leadership theory to comprehend the reasons for the third one. The study also went beyond the limits of bilateral interaction and analyzed the relationship in a regional context by examining in depth and details the views, positions and foreign policy preferences of Turkey and Russia with regard to the main hotspots and problematic areas in the Black Sea, South Caucasus, Central Asia and Middle East.

When writing a book on Turkish–Russian relations the question which occupies the mind constantly is the character of Turkish–Russian interaction, whether the relationship is an example of genuine cooperation or a marriage of convenience that stemmed from shared disappointment with the policies of the USA and the EU. It is clear that both the USA and the EU are important security and economic partners for Turkey and Russia. Both of the countries realize the majority of their trade with EU members; the EU is also the chief investor in various sectors of the Turkish and Russian economies. Moreover, Turkey has been carrying out accession negotiations with the EU since 2005, albeit at a crawling pace and in a convoluted way, and has been aspiring to become a member of the European club for many years. In a similar vein, Turkey and the USA are long-standing allies in NATO, and their military relations are well-rounded and deep-rooted. Russia, on the other hand, had been in fierce competition with the USA over world dominance during the Cold War years and although its fervor and intensity diminished to a great extent in the post-Cold War era, rivalry between the two countries still continues unabated in the regions surrounding Turkey.

The reluctance of some members of the EU to accept Turkey into the European club as an equal member, along with mounting disagreements between Turkey and the USA after Washington's invasion of Iraq, engendered explicit exasperation and distress in Turkey. This situation certainly contributed at some point to the rapprochement with Russia, which had been for a long time feeling growing resentment toward unilateralist American actions, be it Washington's withdrawal from the Anti-Ballistic Missile Treaty or its attack on Iraq with a coalition of the willing without a UN mandate. However, it would be incorrect to reduce the emergence of the advanced level of Turkish–Russian association to both countries' disputes with Brussels and Washington. The warming of relations between Turkey and Russia did not emanate from the joint feelings of frustration, disappointment and uneasiness towards the USA and Europe but came into existence as a result of mutual willingness and determination on the part of Turkish and Russian statesmen and foreign policy-makers whose building blocks were established in the wake of growing economic ties between the two countries in mid-1990s.

In retrospect, it would be true to say that the 1990s had been difficult for both Turkey and Russia as they both had to find their new place in a completely altered world while at the same time having to grapple with serious domestic troubles. The West, including Turkey, came out as victorious from the Cold War. Russia accepted its defeat, acquiesced in the breakup of the Soviet empire, receded from its zones of influence in Central and Eastern Europe and tried to harmonize its political and economic structures with those of the West. However, the Western reform programs and aid packages were not adequate enough to cure Russia's ills, especially while the country was immersed in political instability and economic crises and was also facing the threat of a separatist movement in Chechnya. Furthermore, being the heir of one of the two superpowers, it was not easy for Russia to settle for a second-ranking place in the international arena. So after a baffling period, Russia held onto the last remnants of its defunct empire in the South Caucasus and Central Asia that sheltered many citizens of Russian origin in addition to possessing rich energy resources.

Turkey, on the other hand, despite being part of the winning bloc of the Cold War, realized that with the 'Soviet aggression and communist threat' out of the picture, its influence and privileged position within the Western alliance were shaken considerably. Moreover, intensification of the fight with a separatist Kurdish movement, economic problems and conflicts with neighboring states put Turkey in a difficult and risky position. Ankara wanted to try its chance in the South Caucasus and Central Asia where independent states, with most of whom Turkey shared common historical, ethnic, religious, linguistic and cultural ties, had come on the international scene with the demise of the Soviet Union. This clash of interests between Turkey and Russia triggered a vying for influence in the same regions and brought on competition and confrontation in their relationship at the beginning of the 1990s.

However, it did not take much time for Turkey to become aware of its own limitations and to seek for a rapprochement with Russia in Eurasia, which had proved that it was still the most efficacious player in the region with its explicit and implicit interventions in Nagorno-Karabakh, Abkhazia and South Ossetia and its not so easily erasable impact in Central Asian states sustained through close ties with local political cadres, commercial links and linguistic dominance. Elevating economic and commercial ties between Turkey and Russia also played a crucial role in this period in easing out the tension between the two countries and overcoming the atmosphere of suspicion, mistrust and tension. Turkish contractors, business people and entrepreneurs discovered the large and untapped Russian market, won many bids in the construction sector and realized investments in various industries. The complementary character of the Turkish and Russian economies engendered steady growth in bilateral commerce. Turkey purchased fossil fuels and industrial goods from Russia and in return sold consumer and retail products.

The first signs of genuine moderation and long-lasting accommodation in Turkish–Russian relations came at the beginning of the 2000s when Russia after a period of concern and hesitation commenced to see Turkey not just as a prospective rival but also as a lucrative market for its energy products. Turkey was a perfect client for Russian oil and natural gas exports due to its geographical proximity, growing economy and natural-resource bereft situation. Moreover, a rapprochement with Ankara also promised dividends for Moscow in the political sphere as Turkey, were it to entertain close and cordial relations with Russia, would be less prone to tolerating the activities of Chechen militants and organizations on its territory and would endeavor to strike a fine balance between Washington and Moscow in matters of confrontation and rivalry between these two capitals.

Reaching a compromise with Russia was seen as a positive and important step by the AKP government that took the helm of Turkey at the end of 2002. The new administration had been attaching special importance to the pursuit of a less-conflict ridden and problem-free foreign policy in the immediate neighborhood of Turkey and had been searching for ways to strengthen the country's political and economic ties with the regional states. Russia in this regard occupied a significant place in Turkish foreign policy as a chief energy provider, important trade partner and a global balancer against the unilateral and revisionist encroachments of the USA.

The examination of Turkish–Russian relations in the post-Cold War period attested to the fact that far from being strange bedfellows that ran into each other's arms in defiance of the EU and the USA, Turkey and Russia consciously, deliberately and willingly reached out to each other for a genuine reconciliation in their bilateral association which would offer both of them obvious political and economic benefits. It is also true to say that improving economic relations in particular, expanding collaboration in the field of energy, preceded and facilitated political détente. The opening of a large Russian market for Turkish products, entrepreneurs, and business people in the immediate post-Cold War period and the numerous Turkish investments in the country relaxed the tense and uneasy atmosphere between the two states when the issues such as Nagorno-Karabakh War, Chechen separatism and the Kurdish unrest clouded the political interaction during most of the 1990s. With the rise of Russian natural gas exports to Turkey, accelerated with the construction of the Blue Stream gas pipeline, as well as providing oil and electricity to the Turkish market in large quantities, Russia obtained substantial leverage on Turkey whose effect was clearly observed in the course of the August 2008 war between Georgia and Russia when Turkey chose to adopt a neutral stance and refrained from criticizing Russia despite its close bonds with Georgia. Taking into account the fact that Russian experts would be building the first nuclear plant for Turkey in the coming years, thus enhancing and deepening the energy connection between Russia and Turkey, mutual investments exceeding 20 billion dollars and Russia benefiting from the Turkish Straits for oil transportation prove that the economic side of the Turkish–Russian relationship will preserve its significance in the overall interaction in the coming years. Gaining primacy and the importance of economic issues in Turkish–Russian relations are also in line with the complex interdependency argument that economic matters carry as much as weight as political and security questions for states that are in an interdependent relationship.

Growing and diversifying political and economic relations became possible with bilateral interaction at various levels. In accordance with the premise of complex interdependency theory, Turkey and Russia connect through multiple channels both at governmental and non-governmental spheres. Close contacts at the state and governmental level take place in the form of frequent reciprocal high-profile visits, regular telephone conversations between presidents, premiers and foreign ministers of the two states with respect to bilateral, regional and global issues and setting up of joint working groups that strive for Turkish–Russian accord in various aspects of the relationship. As the theory envisages, the activities and efforts of these small and closed working groups that deal with each other on an intense and regular basis have been crucial for both of the sides to overcome myopic self-interest and to pursue forward-looking policies that focus on overall well-being of the relationship.

As for the non-governmental sphere, the institutions founded by Turkish and Russian business people who create a considerable amount of investments in each other's countries and who act as lobbying mechanisms on governments, the Russian people choosing Turkey for their vacations who brought about mutual awareness and recognition on a people-to-people basis, and finally regular gatherings and the joint work of Turkish and Russian academics also figured largely in the growth of a marked rapport between Ankara and Moscow.

Intensifying political dialogue buttressed by rising economic cooperation did not ensure, however, the adoption of a common outlook and course of action with regard to regional problems in the South Caucasus and Middle East. Far from developing joint projects to resolve regional disputes, political divergence and competition between the two countries endured in these regions. In fact, Turkey and Russia underwent the most severe crisis in their post-Cold War history because of a Middle Eastern crisis, the Syrian civil war which nearly soured every positive aspect of their bilateral relationship. Yet, the seven-month fall-out erupted not only because of collision of interests between the two countries regarding Syria that was triggered due to support for opposite sides in the conflict but also as a result of the growing influence and power of the presidents of Turkey and Russia in foreign policy decision-making.

Erdoğan, who has been investing in the Syrian opposition's cause morally and materially since the outbreak of the conflict, became quite uncomfortable with Russian airstrikes that batted for al-Assad to the detriment of some pro-Turkish fighting groups in Syria. The straw that broke the camel's back, however, became the repeated violations of Turkey's airspace which was taken by Ankara as an encroachment on national sovereignty that must be prevented at all costs even if it included shooting down a Russian jet. Putin, on the other hand, although aware of Turkey's grievances regarding Russia's intervention in Syria to the benefit of al-Assad regime, might probably have not waited for such a fierce reaction from Turkey. Putin's annoyance, furor and disappointment with respect to Erdoğan was put bluntly both through his harsh words directed at Erdoğan and with the severe sanctions he ordered to be imposed on Turkish goods and services.

The increasingly personalized foreign policy decision-making in Turkey and Russia has inflicted severe damage on the relationship. However, economic, social and people-to-people ties threaded meticulously over a quarter of a century were too entrenched and beneficial for both states to easily forgo them. The shuttle diplomacy conducted via the diplomatic staff of Erdoğan and Putin, facilitated with the efforts of the Turkish and Russian business people, has initiated the thaw between Ankara and Moscow that will gradually normalize political relations.

It is well-known that both Erdoğan and Putin first as heads of government then as heads of state contributed to a great extent to the establishment of multifaceted Turkish–Russian relations in the post-Cold War era. Yet their growing power and authority on the domestic political scene which ensured them having a strong impact on foreign policy decision-making induced the two leaders to adopt a belligerent attitude from time to time with regard to some issues as demonstrated in the recent plane crisis between the two countries. In order to anticipate and impede possible future crises and relieve the relationship of whims of strong leaders as much as possible, Turkey and Russia might concentrate on the foundation of common institutions, similar to the BSEC, in areas of shared interest which might help them to solve political disagreements and to minimize the risk of resorting to military confrontation.

The Turkish–Russian interaction, albeit retaining unique and distinct features, does not take place in an isolated environment, and is affected by regional and global developments. In line with this reality, the final pages of this book are devoted to projections about the future status of Turkish–Russian relations, taking into account regional and global dynamics as well as power struggles.

The future of the Syrian state will be crucial with respect to the regional dimension. The political future of al-Assad, the risk of disintegration of the country along ethnic and confessional lines and the struggle against the Islamic State of Iraq and Syria are serious issues that will engross both Turkey and Russia for some time. If Ankara and Moscow come together and succeed in achieving a workable political solution to the Syrian imbroglio by engaging their henchmen in the peace process, it will bring out positive implications both in the bilateral association and for regional stability. The continuance of discord and divergence over Syria, on the other hand, retains the possibility of derailing the newly restored Turkish–Russian rapport.

Another important matter with regard to the regional dimension is the future of the current regime in Iran. Russia will sustain its position of Turkey's number one supplier of energy products as long as Iran is excluded from oil and natural gas projects by Turkey's Western allies. However, a lasting compromise between Iran and the West or a regime change in Iran which will bring to power a new administration that is on better terms with the USA and the EU can open the way for increased energy cooperation between Ankara and Tehran, thus reducing Turkey's dependence on Russian energy supplies. Such a radical development in the region may lead Turkey to become more vocal and persistent in pursuing its interests in the South Caucasus, whereas Russia may feel itself contained and may demonstrate a tougher and more assertive stance in its South Caucasus policy.

At the global level, the increasing competition between the USA and China will have significant implications for the Turkish–Russian relationship. If China continues its economic, military and technological ascendance and comes on to the international scene as a serious rival to American power, then the USA will speed up its efforts to encircle China by entering into alliances with its neighbors and obstructing Beijing's access to energy resources which are vital for the country to fuel its economic growth. While carrying out this mission Washington will most probably seek a compromise with Russia and will strive to draw Moscow to its side in return for some concessions in Eastern Europe, the South Caucasus, Central Asia and the Middle East. Russia may respond to American overtures warmly for the reason that it is quite uneasy and concerned about the expanding and deepening Chinese influence in Central Asia, which expedited after China's inauguration of oil and natural gas pipelines with the Central Asian states that bypassed Russia and broke its monopoly on transit routes for oil and natural gas. China also builds new roads and railways with the aim of directly connecting its territory to Central Asia, thus bolstering its trade with the region. Furthermore, Beijing offers aid programs to Central Asian states, gives support to infrastructure projects such as the construction of hydropower plants and extraction of natural resources, and Chinese firms acquire companies, enter into joint ventures and carry out many investments in Central Asia. With these activities China directly challenges the Russian supremacy and position in the region. Moscow's fears of losing ground to China in Central Asia, coupled with its anxiety about possible Chinese demographic and economic penetration into its sparsely populated Far East region, may make Russia more enthusiastic about taking part in the American policy of encircling China. Such a possible rapprochement between the USA and Russia, though putting Turkey at ease while developing its political, economic and military relations with Russia, may also give rise to a confrontation with a more assertive and demanding Russia, specifically in the South Caucasus region, and may bring about Turkey's retraction from its active and dynamic policy in this area. On the other hand, the USA's preservation of its current superiority may engender a balancing act from China and Russia against US moves in Central Asia, and this situation may put constraints on Turkey while making inroads into the region through economic instruments.

This book has demonstrated that Turkey and Russia have come a long way in transforming their conflictual and confrontational interaction into a cooperative and mutually beneficial one within a quarter of a century. The ascending and diversifying economic collaboration, especially cooperation in the energy field, along with growing interaction at business and people-to-people levels, has paved the way for increasing bilateral contacts and intensified dialogue at the political level.

The remarkable development in political and economic relations, however, did not lead to increased political integration between the two countries. There was not any coordination of policies between Ankara and Moscow regarding the South Caucasian and Middle Eastern matters. As a result they were unable to create common institutions or consultation mechanisms to avert prospective crises or to ensure peaceful and permanent resolution of the conflicts in these regions. Even so, although strong economic ties and growing political interaction were not sufficient to overcome the political divergence in some issue areas, they nevertheless kept the relationship on a solid and steady foundation.

Both Ankara and Moscow value the multifaceted rapport dearly and exert the requisite care and attention to ensure that it is kept on the right track. This was demonstrated again when Russia promptly and unwaveringly stood by the democratically elected government of Turkey in the face of a coup d'état attempt in the country that took place on July 15, 2016 while the USA and the EU were wavering and waiting for the dust to settle down. In return, Russia became the first foreign destination of Turkish President Erdoğan after the averted coup where he and his counterpart President Putin vowed to elevate the relationship. All in all, the Turkish–Russian coupling continues to be one of the most intriguing developments of the post-Cold War era as despite ups and downs and trials and tribulations, the relationship manages to muddle through to a better future.

Index

Abkhazia 7, 37, 47–50, 52, 66, 131
Akkuyu 116, 12
Al-Assad, Bashar 8, 86, 92, 95–7, 133–4
Al-Hariri, Rafiq 93–5
Al-Sisi, Abdel Fattah 89
Aliyev, Heydar 39
Aliyev, Ilham 39, 46–7, 52
August 2008 war 52, 132

Baku-Tbilisi-Ceyhan (BTC) 39, 42, 50, 112
Baku-Tbilisi-Erzurum (BTE) 39, 42, 50
Baku-Tbilisi-Kars (BTK) 42, 50
Basayev, Shamil 78–9
Ben Ali, Zine El Abidine 87
Black Sea Economic Cooperation (BSEC) 11, 41, 66–8, 71–3, 134
Black Sea Forum for Partnership and Dialogue (BSFPD) 71–2
Black Sea Naval Cooperation Task Group (BLACKSEAFOR) 67–8, 72
Blue Stream 20–1, 24, 81, 106, 117, 132; and the construction process 110, 112–13

Caucasus Peace and Stability Pact 36, 51
Caucasus Stability and Cooperation Platform 36, 51
Cem, İsmail 21, 44, 61
Chernomyrdin, Viktor 20, 110, 123n1

Collective Security Treaty Organization (CSTO) 37, 39–40, 46, 59–60
Community of Democratic Choice (CDC) 71–2
Complex interdependency theory 19, 33, 98, 105, 129, 132; and main arguments 2–5
Crimea 8, 66, 68, 70–1, 107
Çavuşoğlu, Mevlüt 71

Davutoğlu, Ahmet 88, 91
Demirel, Süleyman 20–1, 43, 51, 78
Democratic Union Party (PYD) 82
Dudayev, Dzhokhar 77–8

Ecevit, Bülent 80–1
Economic Cooperation Organization (ECO) 36, 58
Elchibey, Abulfaz 39
Erdoğan, Recep Tayyip 2, 20, 22, 28, 29n2, 51, 62, 115, 133–4, 136; and the Arab awakening 88–9, 91, 95, 97; and leadership theory 8–10
Eurasian Economic Community (EurAsEC) 37, 59
Eurasian Economic Union (EEU) 40, 46, 63n3

Foreign Economic Relations Board (DEİK) 106
Free Syrian Army 95

Gaddafi, Muammar 90–2, 97
Gorbachev, Mikhail 38

Gül, Abdullah 44, 90

Hamas 86
Hermann, Charles F. 1
Hezbollah 96
High-Level Russian Turkish Cooperation Council 7, 96

Ivanov, Igor 21, 61, 81

Justice and Development Party (AKP) 21, 90, 95, 131

Kadyrov, Ramzan 82
Kasyanov, Mikhail 81
Keohane, Robert O. 2
Khasavyurt Agreement 77
Khattab, Emir 79
Kurdistan Workers' Party (PKK) 27, 43, 79, 82, 94

Lavrov, Sergey 46, 69, 88–9
Leadership theory 2, 9, 129

Medvedev, Dmitry 22, 52, 82, 116; and the Arab awakening 87, 89; and the Nagorno-Karabakh 40, 46
Minsk Group 38, 53n2
Montreux Convention 51, 65–6, 68–70
Morsi, Mohamed 88–90
Mubarak, Hosni 88–90
Muslim Brotherhood 88–90, 95

Nabucco 47, 114–15
Nagorno-Karabakh 1, 7, 13, 48, 52, 66, 131–2; and the historical background 37–8; and the Russian position 39–40; and the Turkish position 41; and the Turkish-Russian competition 43–47
Nye, Joseph S. 2

Operation Active Endeavor 68, 73n4

Operation Black Sea Harmony 68, 73n3
Öcalan, Abdullah 79, 82, 94
Özal, Turgut 43, 57

Partnership for Peace (PfP) 39, 46, 69
Public Forum 22
Putin, Vladimir 2, 20–2, 25, 29n1, 52, 70, 109, 115, 133–4, 136; and the Arab awakening 89, 96–7; and leadership theory 8–10; and the Nagorno-Karabakh 46

Saakashvili, Mikheil 48, 52, 71
Shanghai Cooperation Organization (SCO) 59–60, 62
South Ossetia 7, 37, 47, 52, 66, 68, 93, 131; and the Russian position 48–9; and the Turkish position 50
South Stream 47, 115
suitcase trade 23, 109
Syria 8, 13, 28, 123, 133–5; and the Turkish-Russian dispute 82–3, 86–7, 92–7
Syrian National Council 95

Trans-Anatolian Natural Gas Pipeline 42, 114
Trans-Caspian Gas Pipeline 112–13
Turkic summits 36, 57, 60
Turkish Cooperation and Coordination Agency (TİKA) 57
Turkish Stream 115
Turkish-Russian Business Council 23, 106
Turkish-Russian Joint Economic Commission 105

Yeltsin, Boris 78–9
Yılmaz, Mesut 20, 113